OPTIONS TRADING

OPTIONS TRADING

JARROTT T. MILLER

Henry Regnery Company · Chicago

Library of Congress Cataloging in Publication Data

Miller, Jarrott T.
    Options trading

    Includes index.
    1. Put and call transactions.   2. Hedging
(Finance)   I. Title.
HG6041.M55   332.6'45   74-32315
ISBN 0-8092-8385-9

Copyright © 1975 by Jarrott T. Miller
All rights reserved
Published by Henry Regnery Company
180 North Michigan Avenue, Chicago, Illinois 60601
Manufactured in the United States of America
Library of Congress Catalog Card Number: 74-32315
International Standard Book Number: 0-8092-8385-9

Published simultaneously in Canada by
Fitzhenry & Whiteside Limited
150 Lesmill Road
Don Mills, Ontario M3B 2T5
Canada

Contents

Illustrations and Tables

Preface

An option is the privilege of demanding fulfillment of a contract on any day within a specified time. In most business situations, this right to choose costs the option seeker money. The option grantor requires this payment in return for his granting the privilege.

The choice purchased by the option owner may be to buy a building, a piece of land, or a stock. The choice may also be to sell some valuable possession. In all cases, the price at which the article will be bought or sold is agreed upon at the time the option agreement is made. The only unspecified element is that the option owner may demand fulfillment of his contract on any day, either sooner or later, up to the day the option expires.

The options industry has had a long and invariably controversial history. Until just recently, dealings in options were private, or at least semiprivate, usually involving persons of wealth and financial sophistication. However, with the establishment of the Chicago Board Options Exchange, the first continuous marketplace for stock options, all the advantages of options are now easily within the grasp of the whole investing public.

Unfortunately, the financial press, in its coverage of the options business, has fostered a prejudicial attitude toward options buyers. "Option writers," it is said, are "either institutions or sagacious individuals of wealth acting wisely and prudently; option buyers," by the same argument, are "rank speculators, gamblers, or at least uninformed fools." By this logic, the dynamic growth of the options business is attended by a disproportionate increase of horse's asses among the public.

Of course, the truth of the matter is that many option speculators *are* artless wishful thinkers who persist in the hope of getting a free lunch. Back at the turn of the century, they disgorged their millions in the bucket shops. Bucket shops were the illegitimate face of the legitimate Member Firm Brokerage Houses. A handy store front, a little money spent on decor and the wages of a few clerks—and an operator was in business.

When a customer walked into a bucket shop, it looked like the real thing. The clerks would be busy changing the current prices of stocks listed on a large blackboard. A ticker tape clacking out the price quotes from the New York Stock Exchange would be close at hand. The tape and the board were the center of interest for the lounging observers. As soon as the customer decided which stock he wanted to "purchase," he would place an order at the cashier's cage and put up ten percent of the price, in theory borrowing the balance. He received a receipt noting the current price of the stock, the number of shares, and the amount of margin money paid. The order to buy went into the wastebasket, *i.e.,* it was "bucketed." In fact, the customer was betting that the stock would go up and the house was betting against him. If it did go up, the customer would present his receipt to the cashier and receive the new price of his shares less commissions and the amount of his "loan." Should the price decline, the customer would get a call to put up more margin. If he failed to do so (and about all customers did), his position would be wiped out and the shop would keep his money. He had lost his bet.

By dealing with bucket shops, the speculator could at least limit his risk. The bucket shops never came after his bank account for more margin. They just pocketed his original bet along with those of thousands of other crapshooters. On the other hand, if he happened to make a killing, he might also find his favorite bucket shop had reverted into an empty store front overnight, the operator having taken the night train to the next town.

Speculation has always been with us and always will be. Sometimes it serves an economic and social purpose, other times not. However, for the individual the most important distinction is whether his speculations are stupid or wise. There is a great body of intelligent speculators who are aware of the potential advantages of buying options compared to other forms of out-and-out crapshooting in the stock market. This book is addressed to these prudent speculators and would-be speculators.

No aspect of financial analysis has been so ignored as that of option buying. The industry has blithely assumed that the population consists of an inexhaustible supply of suckers who will buy whatever is offered. However, a healthy, sturdy options industry will only prosper when all the participants are equally well informed. If the sheep don't get smart, even the wolves will go hungry.

My most valuable critic during the preparation and execution of this work has been Mr. Robert Jackson. Bob's questions and ideas have made the most important single contribution. In addition, I would like to thank Laurence A. Mitchell, Jr., of Goldman, Sachs & Co.; Gerald Goldsmith of E. F. Hutton & Co.; and Gary Mayer of Bache & Co. for their astute insights into the option market. Marc Thompson deserves my gratitude for his suggestions and help in running down pertinent historical references. Above all, my wife, Diane, merits my greatest appreciation for diligently aiding me with the drudgery of typing and editing.

OPTIONS TRADING

1

Options: Past to Present

THE business section of your local bookstore will seldom have less than three and often many more titles dealing with options. The financial newspapers and periodicals are equally well stocked with advertisements for options services. Invariably, the thrust of all this effort is to make you more knowledgeable about *writing* options. The purpose of this book is to point out the advantages of *buying* options both on the Over-the-Counter market and the Chicago Board Options Exchange. Techniques for selecting the most highly leveraged and least risky options will be disclosed. The strategies of outright purchase, option trading, and option hedging will be discussed. All in all, this book should benefit the occasional speculator, the serious trader, and even the most intractable option writer. Before getting enmeshed in the specifics, let's take a brief look at the evolution of the option.

Few realize that options have been used in commerce since

biblical times. For the student, their history is fascinating. For the more practical minded, a knowledge of the antecedents of our present options business will point out some of the more imaginative ways in which these remarkably versatile tools can be used.

Aristotle wrote in his *Politics* that the ancient philosopher Thales made a fortune through the clever use of options. Being a careful observer as well as a thinker, Thales concluded that the next year's olive crop in Miletus would be very bountiful. Since a philosopher's pay was no better then than today, he sought to capitalize on his judgment and leverage his funds. He procured options on virtually every olive press in the district for the next harvest season and effectively "cornered the market." When the bumper crop arrived, he leased out the presses at exorbitant rates and thus secured his fortune.

The option with which Thales dealt was a good skeleton but lacked some of the flesh of its more refined offspring. Basically, an option is a right. The option seller grants a right to do something. The option buyer pays money to the seller to receive that right. The money that changes hands is called the option money or option premium. In commerce, the right is usually the right to buy or sell an article at a price agreed upon at the time the option is entered into. Usage has established that the name of the option is determined by the nature of the right viewed from the buyer's standpoint. If the buyer pays his option money so that he can take something from the seller at the agreed upon price, the option is termed a call. If the buyer's right is to give something to the seller, the option is called a put. (Interestingly enough, in contemporary England, calls are referred to as takes and puts as gives.) The last element of an option is one of time. Since a specific amount of money is paid for the option, the option normally only lasts for a specific length of time. This is also agreed to when the option is bought. If the option buyer chooses not to exercise his right, the right will expire. The option seller or grantor is richer by the premium. Presumably, the option buyer chose to forfeit his option right because of some other economic justification.

The first sophisticated use of options in history occurred during the legendary tulip-bulb craze in 17th-century Holland. In the 1630s the Dutch became so enamored of tulips that the prices of the bulbs began to rise by leaps and bounds. At the onset those in the trade used options for hedging. A dealer with a forward sales commitment would buy sufficient calls to assure that he would have the necessary bulbs at a set price when he had to deliver the physical product. On the other hand, tulip-bulb growers would buy put options to guarantee a market at a set price for their product. However, as the mania really took hold, speculators rushed to buy calls as the most profitable vehicle to wealth for the least amount of capital. As prices spiraled upwards, the owners of the calls made more money than the speculators who bought the bulbs themselves. Virtually all commerce in Holland ceased, save the trading in tulip bulbs and related paper.

Legend has it that a visiting sailor triggered the "coup de theatre" by inadvertantly lunching on a $10,000 tulip bulb, thinking it to be an onion.

This instance of folk wisdom might have put the inflated prices into perspective. More likely, the reality that the handful of frenzied spendthrifts willing to pay a king's ransom for a single bulb could hardly digest the hundreds of thousands of tubers that Holland grew caused complete disintegration of the trade. The subsequent economic depression lasted for decades in Holland. Speculators who had spent their life savings buying calls on the economically useless bulbs were ruined. Put writers, either unable or unwilling to pay out their fortunes for the bulbs put to them, went bankrupt. Options, so intimately involved in the craze and the collapse that followed, acquired a bad name that is still with us today.

In our own country, trading in puts (contracts to sell stock at a fixed price for a set period of time) and calls (contracts to buy stock at a specified price for a set time interval) had been used by sophisticated and professional traders since the inception of the securities market. However, it was not until the 1860s that options trading became widespread. One man, Russell Sage, became the propelling and dominating force in the options business.

Russell Sage

Sage arrived on Wall Street with a hoard of capital accumulated from a variety of commodity and shipping enterprises. He promptly put his money to work at very profitable interest rates. The insatiable demand for capital and loans during this period of the nation's commercial expansion soon made him an extremely wealthy man. One of his largest sources of income arose from lending money to great personages for their various stock acquisitions and manipulations.

Sage's career as a banker was interrupted when he was indicted in 1869 for lending money at usurious rates. Although defended by several prominent politicians who had benefited over the years by his loans, he prudently decided to disguise the "same old business" with a new face. Sage was a master speculator who saw a plethora of opportunity where lesser men saw nothing. Truly, he could have sold long-john underwear in the Fiji Islands.

His first innovation was the "conversion," an invention of true genius. When approached by a client who wanted to borrow money to buy stock, Sage accommodated his client using options, or "privileges" as they were then known. First he would demand a *free* put from the eager client. Next he would purchase 100 shares of the object stock, and then in turn *sell* a call to the client. Should the stock decline, he could put the shares to the client and so be protected. Should the stock rise, the client, by exercising his call at the lower option price would derive the full benefit. Regardless of the fate of the stock, Sage could neither make nor lose capital. His profit came from selling the call and the State of New York had no usury laws governing the sale of calls.

The client, by giving a put and buying a call, had all the advantages and attendent risks of owning the stock outright. Obliquely, Sage still maintained his usurious lending business;

his clients achieved their speculative purposes, and the New York Attorney General had to seek other, less wily game.

Sage's inventive turn didn't stop with conversions. He then went on with "straddles" and "spreads." A straddle is a combination of a put and a call, each having the same striking price. A spread is a straddle wherein the component put and call are at different striking prices. Sage devised most of the elements of the modern options business. His contributions earned him the title of "Father of Puts and Calls" and alternatively "Old Straddle."

Having forged the tools, Sage was no slouch in their profitable deployment. However, he shunned the public eye. Many of his deals depended upon the confidentiality of the transactions for their success. Consequently, some of the more famous and infamous market operators received credit for spectacular manipulations that rightfully belonged to Sage. Sage never took umbrage. He was fully satisfied with profit.

Russell Sage, like all men at the forefront of an enterprise that attracts public scrutiny, was quick to justify his activities in the most favorable light. He first revealed that he "had entered the occult business of option writing to help out small brokers who wished to operate on his huge capital."[1]

One might question Sage's espoused generosity considering that he could exert substantial influence on the market. If a particular stock's price movement was not to his benefit, he certainly had the wherewithal to make the price do his bidding.

Secondly, Sage contended that "since the purchasers of said puts, calls, straddles, etc., could never lose more than the premium cost of those options, he [Sage] provided the 'poor man' with a chance to profit from the price movements of 'blue chips' in the same manner as the rich man who could maintain a margin account—only without any risk over and above the option's cost to the purchaser."[2]

---

1. Paul Sarnoff, *Russell Sage: The Money King,* p. 237.

2. Sarnoff, *Russell Sage: The Money King,* p. 237.

Sage's observation of the facts was absolutely correct, although his implication that he wanted to benefit the "poor man" had more than a small touch of hypocrisy.

Sage also recommended certain strategies for using options. For all the color that surrounded his life he was above all a very conservative, though unorthodox, financier. He seldom really took risks. By writing options on stocks he virtually controlled, he avoided risk. His adroit handling of the conversion was foolproof. It was Russell Sage, The Master, who stated that the only sensible way to trade a market was to use a call to protect a short sale and a put to protect a long position.

The Contemporary Options Market

The days of the "lawful" manipulators have come and gone. This isn't to say that there still aren't any unscrupulous entrepreneurs around looking for an opportunity. As long as wealth is portable, e.g., currency bank balances, bonds, stocks, etc., as opposed to the more cumbersome varieties, e.g., cattle, wives, stone wheels, etc., some shrewd fellow will find a way to convey the public's money into his pocket, the law be hanged. Witness the escapades of Anthony De Angelis, Billy Sol Estes, Bernie Cornfeld, Robert Vesco, et al.

Regardless of those who might occasionally abuse legitimate business, the options business has grown manyfold since the days of Russell Sage. According to a 1961 SEC study, sales of options increased from 0.49 percent of the NYSE volume in 1943 to 1.12 percent in 1960. In June of 1959, the number of options outstanding (presently called open interest—a term borrowed from the commodities futures industry) covered some 3,700,000 shares of stock.

Several developments have occurred in recent years that have dramatically heightened the interest and enlarged the scope of options trading even further. The first was the introduction of the Down-and-Out option. The second, and most important, was the establishment of the Chicago Board Options Exchange.

Down-and-Outers

Early in the 1970s, several brokerage houses—Goldman Sachs, Donaldson, Lufkin & Jenrette, Bear Stearns, and Oppenheimer— began marketing a new kind of option. In Street jargon, it was called the "down-and-outer." The idea behind presenting this new product was to offer an option that would give a "fairer shake" to the buyer.

The first of the special features of the "down-and-outer" (the proper technical name is "special expiration price option") bene- fits the writer. These options have an *expiration price* as well as the usual expiration date. In the case of a call, if the price of the common under option falls to the expiration price, the call auto- matically expires. If the option is a put (some brokerage houses do make a market in "up-and-outers") and the price of the optioned stock advances to the expiration price, the put expires. The purpose is to let the option writer off the financial hook if his underlying position deteriorates. The call writer is not required to hold a plummeting stock, nor is a put writer obliged to hold a skyrocketing short. With the option automatically cancelled, the writer can bail out and completely free his capital as well.

As an example, if a six-month-and-ten-day "down-and-out" call were bought on a $40 stock, the expiration date would be six months and ten days hence. The expiration price would be around $36. The usual "out" price is 10 percent below the strike price for a call and 10 percent above for a put. If the stock never fell to 36, the option would expire in a little over six months. Otherwise sooner.

What advantage would induce buyers to purchase options which could possibly expire overnight? The greatest of all—cheap- ness. Down-and-outers are sold for just about half the price of the usual OTC option. Whereas the cost of a six-month option usually amounts to 20 percent of the cost of the underlying stock, "down- and-outs" can be bought for a little more than half that amount.

Low cost is not the only feature used to attract buyers. These options have a rebate feature that amounts to a kind of resale market. If the buyer chooses to exercise the option before the expiration date, he will receive a pro-rata share of his option money back. On a six month option, this would amount to a one-sixth rebate per month. Thus, if the option were exercised at the end of one month, $\frac{5}{6}$ of the option cost would be rebated; if at the end of three months, one half. Consequently, it can be advantageous to exercise an unprofitable option just to get part of the option cost back. Some return on a bad option is a lot better than a dead loss.

The brokerage houses that write and market the "down-and-outers" and "up-and-outers" have deliberately chosen to maintain a very low profile. Only favored clients are solicited for the business. For subtle schizophrenic reasons, the houses that introduced these special options don't really want to be very closely associated with the options business. The rationale seems to be that what is respectable with a high class clientele is disreputable with the public. Since antiquity, the most successful madames have operated their businesses on just such a basis.

The Chicago Board Options Exchange

Established in April 1973, as an offshoot of the Chicago Board of Trade, the world's largest commodity futures trading market, the CBOE has been the most significant innovation in options since Russell Sage's day.

In November 1973, the sales volume of options had increased to more than 6 percent of the New York Stock Exchange volume. The new business on the CBOE accounted for the lion's share of this startling increase. By March 1974, the CBOE monthly trading volume had further increased to 33.6 million shares, equivalent to 11 percent of *all* the shares traded during the month on the NYSE. *Fortune* estimated that the September 1973 CBOE option volume was equal to 60 percent of the volume of the underlying stock traded on the NYSE. By May 1974, this figure had bounded to 121.2 percent of the equivalent NYSE volume. It is also quite likely that the call options outstanding on the CBOE might surge to more than 100,000,000 shares of underlying stock before 1974 is out, if there is a renewed bull market. Such an open interest would represent nearly 4 percent of the total shares outstanding of the 32 companies on which options were traded in November 1973. The "trial run" for a call option market allowed by the SEC seems to be a whopping success.

Because of the unique features of the CBOE options, the trading characteristics of this market, as opposed to the conventional over-the-counter market, will be described in an entirely different section.

2

Over-the-Counter Options

As mentioned earlier, the original option market was a completely private affair. The option writer and the option buyer sat down face to face and individually negotiated the terms. To understand the essence of the negotiation, one must understand the viewpoints of the two parties.

Usually the option writer who originated and personally guaranteed the option was a financially sound individual who wished to earn extra income on the stocks in his portfolio. If the option was a call and the stock rose in value, the writer would have the stock called away from him at any time during the life of the option, be paid the strike price for his shares, and keep the option money for his troubles. Writing calls on securities already owned is termed writing "covered" options. The call buyer who called the stock away could secure his profit by reselling the shares at the higher market price. If the price declined below the strike

11

price, the call buyer or owner would not exercise or call the stock because there would be no profit in calling a stock that could be bought cheaper on the open market. The call writer would keep his depreciated stock but would also have the option money to offset part or possibly all of the loss of capital value.

If the call writer had sufficient financial resources, he might occasionally write calls "naked," i.e., without owning the stock optioned. In this case, the writer is actually betting against the buyer that the stock won't advance. If the writer wins, the option money paid to him is pure risk profit. As a bonus, he doesn't have to carry a deteriorating stock. However, if the stock advanced, the naked call writer might face the possibility of having to buy the appreciated shares to deliver to the call owner at a much lower price. Writing naked calls can be both very profitable and equally hair-raising—for all purposes almost identical to selling a stock short.

The operation of a put option is almost the exact reverse of the mechanics of the call. The put writer can sell short the stock on which he grants the put option to the buyer. If the stock declines, the writer is obligated to accept the shares put to him and pay the higher option strike price. His profit from the short sale will offset the cost of having to pay over the current market for the shares put to him.

However, this approach is not very conservative if the stock price rises. The put buyer will not exercise his option, for there would be no profit in putting a high-priced stock at a lower option strike price. However, the writer would be stuck with his short sale running away from him.

From the put writer's standpoint, the most conservative approach is to write naked puts on stocks that he wants to own and doesn't mind paying over the market to own. The loss of having to pay over the market price can never be as great as the possible loss of having to cover a runaway short sale.

Of course, an alternative to either writing covered or naked would be to work with stop orders. The naked call writer could place a buy stop order to purchase the optioned shares if the price starts to rise. On the other hand, the covered call writer could place a stop to sell out his underlying shares if the price drops, and thereby go naked.

The naked put writer could sell short the underlying shares if the price starts down. The covered put writer could, conversely, place a stop to buy in his short position if the stock starts to rise. The disadvantages of a writer trying to second-guess the market direction is that short-term price movements can whip-saw the hell out of an overly cautious writer. Experience indicates that the most profitable long-term writing strategy is to write a diversity of covered calls and naked puts on carefully selected securities.

The intricacies of options are much different from the buyer's standpoint. Usually, the purchaser is a speculator seeking almost pure price appreciation. Consequently, he is extremely concerned about buying his option for the lowest price. The less he pays for his option, the less money he has at risk and the better leverage for profits if all works out as he expects. He could care less about whether the writer wrote naked or covered or uses protective stops or not. If he bought a call, he wants the price to rise. If he bought a put, he wants the price to plummet. As opposed to the writer who calculates how to defend his capital from undue risk, the intelligent buyer devotes his energy to making the most out of his limited investment. Since this book focuses on option buying, almost all that follows will be from the buyer's point of view.

As the interest in options became more widespread, an over-the-counter (OTC) market was formed. This market for the most part supplanted the need for face-to-face negotiations and therefore enabled buyers and writers in different parts of the country to make deals. Two developments made this possible. The first grew out of the force of custom. Convention had established that a single option would always cover 100 shares, even though any theoretical number was possible. Also, the length of time the option would run was generally standardized at 30-day, 60-day, 90-day, 6-month-&-10-day, and 1-year intervals. The expiration date was set at one of these intervals from the day the agreement was made. These conventions greatly simplified the number of problems that had to be resolved in coming to terms.

The second development was the emergence of a trade group that specialized in options. Practically all orders for the purchase and sale of OTC options are executed in New York by members of the Put and Call Brokers and Dealers Association, Inc. This association, consisting of approximately 20 members, is a self-regulated organization that deals exclusively in options. Each option firm acts as a broker—a middleman—to bring an agreeable buyer and seller together. Income results from transaction commissions as well as any profits from the option inventory maintained to service customers.

Most importantly, each option is guaranteed by a member firm of the New York Stock Exchange. Since an option buyer pays cash when he buys an option contract, this side of a contract needs no assurances. On the other hand, the seller (or writer) of the option promises to perform an obligation (either buy or sell 100 shares of stock) any time during the duration of the option in return for the money he receives (the premium) for the option. The member firm (almost all medium-to-large brokerage firms are members of the NYSE) guarantees that its customer—the customer who wrote the option—will perform on his contract whether it is profitable or not. This guarantee of performance is the hinge pin between reputable business and the bucket shop. In order to protect this guarantee, the brokerage houses keep a close eye on the customers they allow to write options, and usually have fairly stringent capital requirements for such customers.

A few years ago one major brokerage house allowed too many undercapitalized customers to write naked call options, i.e., writing calls without buying the underlying stock. The market subsequently rose to such an extent that many of the customers refused to buy in the stock to deliver to the option holders. The house that had guaranteed the options stood good on the transactions, but the capital drain was so severe that it was forced into a shotgun merger with a financially sound competitor. The financial criterion for option writers has since been substantially upgraded.

As already stated, an OTC option contract is individually negotiated between buyer and seller with a Put and Call Broker-Dealer acting as an intermediary. Generally, the strike price or price at which the option is set is the price of the underlying stock on the day the option contract is entered into, although in some instances the option contract might specify some other strike price. A call where the strike price is below the prevailing underlying stock price, or a put where the strike price is above the current stock price, is called an "in-the-money" option. A call where the strike price is above the current stock price, or a put where the strike price is below the stock price, is an "out-of-the-money" option. If the contract is a straddle (one put and one call on the same stock), the strike price will be the same for each leg of the double option. A variation of the straddle is the "spread," where each component of the double option has a different strike price.

The price of the option, or option money (usually referred to as the premium) is the principal bargaining point. When a buyer is interested in an option on a particular stock, he can check the ads in the *Wall Street Journal, Barron's,* or the *New York Times* to see what is offered by the option dealers themselves. Whether or not he finds anything interesting in these sources, he should also check with his stock broker. Since not all brokerage houses are active in OTC options, he should obviously be doing business only with a house that is option-oriented. Most NYSE member firms are. When a buyer gets a quote from his broker, he can either accept it or counter with a lower bid.

These negotiations usually take place over the phone or tele-type. In some cases, the broker's put and call department can haggle with a put and call dealer who is willing to sell the option out of his inventory. In other cases, either the broker's put and call department or the put and call dealer will be in direct contact with an investor willing to write the option. If the prospective buyer thinks the price is too high and counters with a lower bid, he has no assurance that it will be accepted. In fact, if too much time is lost in fiddling, the original offer to sell the option might be withdrawn. This is particularly true if the option desired is very popular, or events are moving rapidly. Such are the problems of trying to put deals together over long distance.

As a guideline, option writers seek an annualized return from their option writing activities of between 25 to 40 percent. As one might expect, the writer demands a higher return, and therefore a higher premium, for writing on the more volatile speculative issues, and will settle for a lower return for writing on the less volatile, less risky investment grade stocks. The overall tone of the market and the underlying stock in particular will have a bearing on option prices. In a falling market, the prices of calls tend to decline and the prices of puts tend to rise. The converse is true in rising markets.

Since options are always on 100 shares of stock, the prices are again, by convention, quoted in points per share under option. As an example, a 6-month-&-10-day call option on Combustion Engineering stock at 96 might be offered at $11\frac{7}{8}$. That means that the call would cost the buyer $11\frac{7}{8}$ per share or $1,187.50 for the whole 100-share option. You will also note that all fractional prices are always stated in multiples of $\frac{1}{8}$ point, just as are the prices on the underlying stock. If the price is low enough, 1/16 of a point is sometimes used. Since commissions are involved, the option seller receives $\frac{3}{8}$ of a point less than what the buyer pays. $\frac{1}{8}$ point goes to the buyer's stock broker, $\frac{1}{8}$ point goes to the broker's put-and-call dealer, and $\frac{1}{8}$ point goes to the seller's stock broker.

An OTC option confers virtually all the benefits of stock ownership on the holder of the option. If the stock on which the holder has an option were to split 2 for 1, the option terms would be appropriately modified, i.e., each option would increase from 100 shares to 200 shares. Similarly, if a dividend is paid on the optioned stock, the strike price of the option is reduced by a like amount. For the holder of a call on the stock, the effect is to give the dividend to the option holder if he exercises the option. Just as the short seller is liable to pay any dividends to the person from whom he has borrowed the stock to sell short, the reduction of the strike price for a put holder serves the same purpose. Of course, if the options are not exercised, the call holder doesn't receive the dividend and the put holder doesn't have to pay it since the adjustment is made via the alteration of the strike price.

This subject brings up the whole topic of what to do with the option once you own it. As is true with securities, the disposition is frequently more critical than the acquisition. With OTC options, this problem is even more complex because of the ephemeral life of the option and the very limited resale possibilities.

The only time an option buyer can be assured of a resale market for an OTC option is just before its expiration. If the option is worthless because it has no intrinsic value (say, a call on GM at 80 when the common is at 50), the brokerage house with whom you do business will buy the option from you for $1. The broker performs this as a service for his customer. Obviously, he has no other reason. The customer, by disposing of his worthless option at some price, can clearly establish the date of his capital loss for tax purposes.

More happily, should the option owner's judgment have been sound and the option approaches expiration with a profit, he has two alternatives. Let's take the case of a speculator who, having bought one call on Natomas at 45 for $525, gleefully watches Natomas bounce to 55 as his call approaches expiration. At this point, the call has an intrinsic value of $1,000. He can exercise his call—buy NOM at 45—and then resell the stock on the open market at 55. He will pay a commission of approximately $67 to his broker to buy the 100 shares at 45 and then pay another commission of approximately $75 when he resells his 100 shares at 55. Consequently, the whole cost of the option transaction is the cost of the option of $525 plus the two commissions ($67 plus $75 or $142) for a total of $667. Since the gross profit is (55−45) times 100 shares or $1,000, the net is $333. This is a return of 63 percent on the original investment of $525.

The transaction would be classified as a short-term capital gain for tax purposes since the stock was purchased and sold the same day. The cost of the option and subsequent commission costs would be added to the purchase price basis of the stock. One could get a long-term capital gains treatment by exercising the option and then holding the stock for more than six months before selling it.

The alternative to exercising the option to realize the profit would be to sell the "in-the-money" option outright. Here again, the customer's broker will usually buy the option from his customer. If the option is a profitable call held longer than six months, selling the option itself at a profit will establish a long-term capital gain for the option holder. The broker will then in turn exercise the option and charge the customer the same two commissions as if he had done the job himself. The only advantage is the tax benefit. However, this advantage is quite meaningful if the option is a put, since this technique is the only way that a long-term capital gain can be realized from anything resembling a short sale.

The foregoing is not meant to imply that there is *no* secondary resale market for OTC options. Most of the large dealers will occasionally buy profitable options that still have considerable life left. However, this limited resale market is not large and is pretty much confined to the most popular options. These options are in turn resold as "special" options by the dealer. In those cases where the original option buyer has a profit and resells to a dealer, the commission cost is only the same ⅜ of a point normally charged when the option was first written. This is quite a cost advantage when compared to the double commission cost on the underlying stock charged to exercise. Nonetheless, you should never buy an OTC option with the idea that you will be assured of a resale opportunity.

There is one other special situation in which there is a possibility of resale of a profitable option. If the option customer has had a long and favorable experience with his broker, the broker will under certain conditions, and only as a service to the customer, buy a profitable *put* option from the customer. (Unfortunately, this service does not apply to calls.) The broker then "converts" the put. He buys 100 shares of the underlying stock and sells a call. Because the public interest is always skewed towards the long, optimistic buy side, calls usually command a better price than puts. In buying the cheap put and selling the more expensive call, there is sufficient money left over to pay the interest charges on the money borrowed to buy the 100 shares of stock. The broker is now long 100 shares of stock, long one put, and short one call. The broker is completely secure in his conversion. If the stock drops, he can put the stock he bought to the original put seller and the call will go unexercised. If the stock price rises, he will let the put expire and deliver the bought stock over to the call buyer. The broker is completely hedged. This is the same technique that Russell Sage used, except that he got his puts free instead of paying for them.

However, when the interest rates on money get to the 10 percent level, very few brokers will do any conversions because the difference between the put and call prices is not enough to pay the interest charges on the money borrowed to buy the stock.

Given that a resale market cannot be counted on except close to the expiration date—and only rarely any other time—the usual method of capturing profit is by exercising the option. Under the terms of the option agreement, the option can be exercised at *any* time during its life. Most option buyers, however, tend *not* to exercise until the last minute. Their rationale is that they bought time and don't want to squander any of their option by premature exercise. Often they will hold on even though their best judgment tells them that the underlying stock's move has peaked out. This potential dilemma will be covered later in the section on option hedging.

With these fundamentals of the OTC market under the

belt, we will now move on to study concrete situations involving the profitable purchase of options. First we will look at buying calls, then buying puts. In both cases, we'll analyze the disadvantages as well as the advantages compared to other ways of participating in the anticipated price movement. Then we'll investigate the ins and outs of straddle strategy, wherein combinations of stock and options come into play. The importance of timing will be most evident in this section. Finally, we'll delve into option hedging. In this activity, the speculator can either start out as a crapshooter and wind up a conservative, or start out as a conservative and stay that way.

Buying Calls

While options can be used for purposes both conservative and speculative, by far the greatest number of option buyers are basically gamblers. As the old saying goes, "They pays their money and they takes their chances." Just as in Las Vegas, a definite sum of money is put up in the expectation of the possibility of a ˈastly greater return.

Unlike his Las Vegas brethren, however, the option buyer actually buys control over the capital he is betting on. In everyday terms, anyone who borrows money does the same thing. In the case of a borrower, the price paid for control is the interest charge.

In buying a mortgaged house, the home owner gets all the advantages of a house that was partially paid for with someone else's money. If the value of the house appreciates, the owner reaps the profit, not the lender. Unfortunately, such an advantage seldom accrues if one borrows money to buy an automobile. For better or worse, the idea of deriving all the benefits of money one doesn't have but can borrow is the mainspring of the whole economy of the United States. The buyer risks the money he puts down as a down payment. The lender takes a somewhat lesser risk in return for the charges he assesses.

Also unlike gamblers in Las Vegas—where the bet is placed in the face of certain mathematical odds that dictate the probable outcome—the option buyer is doing more than just playing the odds. He's playing his judgment and experience in the market. He is gambling that he can predict the outcome based on his interpretation of facts, actions and reactions, opinions, and all the myriad forces that interact in the marketplace. While this is gambling of a sort, it is a lot more sophisticated and complicated than pulling the arm on a slot machine.

Let's look at an example that will put these elements of leverage, risk, and gambling in concrete terms. In 1971 the market was struggling upwards toward recovery after its disastrous 1969-1970 plunge. In October, 1971, one-year calls on Ampex at 15 were offered for $350. Considering that the one-year premium was only 23 percent of the stock price for a company like Ampex, the call looked like a bargain. Ampex, a leading manufacturer of magnetic tape equipment and associated sophisticated electronic devices, had always been a volatile stock. At 15, it was way down from the previous year's high of 25. There were some clouds over the company's immediate earning prospects. Yet Ampex enjoyed an excellent reputation for quality and technological superiority of its products.

The cost of acquisition of 100 shares of APX common stock could be approached three possible ways: outright purchase for cash, buying on margin, or using the call option. Obviously the cash cost of 100 shares at 15 was $1,500. At the time of the example, the initial margin requirement was 55 percent. Thus, to buy APX on margin, 55 percent of $1,500, or $825, would be the required down payment with the balance of $675 borrowed from the broker. The cheapest way, of course, to take advantage of an APX rebound would be by buying the option for $350.

Unfortunately, in the next few months various discrepancies were discovered in Ampex's accounting practices and the stock headed southward. Within a year it was down more than 50 percent to 6½. Table 1 shows how each prospective buyer would have fared.

TABLE 1

Buying Ampex with Subsequent Downturn
(All figures in dollars unless noted otherwise)

Buyer Type	Price @ 15			Price @ 6½			Loss	Loss (%)
	Market Value	Debit Balance	Cash Equity	Market Value	Debit Balance	Cash Equity		
Cash	1,500	—	1,500	650	—	650	−850	57
Margin	1,500	675	825	650	675	−25	−850	81
Option	—	—	350	—	—	—	−350	100

The cash investor saw his investment erode by the amount that the price dropped. The margin buyer would have come out much worse. When one buys on margin he must maintain a minimum equity in his account of 30 percent of the market value of the margined stock. With APX at 6½, the market value of the 100 shares would be $650. 30 percent of $650 is $195. However, the equity in the account—the market value of the stock ($650) less the amount borrowed from the broker when the stock was bought (a debit balance of $675)—is a minus $25. Consequently, a margin call would have been issued requesting that the customer put up enough money to cover the deficit of $25 plus another $195 (a total of $220) to maintain the position at the minimum margin level. This new investment in the margin account would bring the total to $825 plus $220, or $1,045. Of this total, the equity of only $195 would remain for a loss of $1,045 less $195, or $850. This is a loss of 81 percent of the original and subsequent margin investment.

The option buyer paid his $350 and lost his whole investment when he let his call expire.

Who fared the best? On a percentage basis, the cash buyer took the least beating. On the other hand, both the cash and margin buyers lost the most money. Actually, the margin buyer lost the most money on a percentage basis considering that he lost all his original investment and had to put up even more money to meet his margin call. Overall, the option buyer lost the least money on the venture, regardless of his high percentage loss. In effect, he had the least exposure to risk in the event of a mistake in judgment. However, the margin and cash buyers did have one significant advantage. They had the opportunity to cut their loss by selling out as the price of APX dropped. The holder of the OTC call could only ride his loss down with remorse.

Let's now look at the other side of the coin by hypothesizing that Ampex had had its anticipated recovery and rose to 25 in one year's time.

TABLE 2

Buying Ampex with Subsequent Upturn
(All figures in dollars unless noted otherwise)

Buyer Type	Price @ 15			Price @ 25			Gain	Gain (%)
	Market Value	Debit Balance	Cash Equity	Market Value	Debit Balance	Cash Equity		
Cash	1,500	—	1,500	2,500	—	2,500	1,000	67
Margin	1,500	675	825	2,500	675	1,825	1,000	123
Option	—	—	350	1,000	—	1,000	650	186

As in the previous instance, both the cash and margin buyers realized the same dollar change in market value since they both held the same number of shares. Of course, the margin buyer earned a higher percentage profit because he was working with borrowed money.

As before, the option buyer started with an equity of $350 and, presuming no resale market for an option having no intrinsic value, a market value of zero. With the advance of APX to 25, the market value of the option to buy 100 shares at 15 is $1,000. The profit would be this market value less the $350 cost, or $650. This represents a return on investment of 186 percent, the highest of the three methods of participating in the APX price advance.

TABLE 3

Summary of Ampex Price Movement

Buyer Type	Initial Total Investment (15)	Loss APX @ 6½		Initial Total Investment @ 15	Gain APX @ 25	
	($)	($)	(%)	($)	($)	(%)
Cash	1,500	850	57	1,500	1,000	67
Margin	1,045	850	81	825	1,000	123
Option	350	350	100	350	650	186

The summary in Table 3 outlines the advantages and disadvantages of both option and margin trading compared to outright ownership in a widely swinging market. When there is a large possibility of an unexpected downside movement, the purchase of a call option is very conservative in terms of minimizing dollar risk. As can be seen, the purchase on margin is the most speculative mode, since a falling market will actually suck the buyer deeper into his predicament because of margin calls. On the other hand, both cash and margin buyers can cut their losses by liquidation if they so choose.

If one's judgment of the anticipated price movement is correct, the call option markedly outpaces any other approach. For nearly the same dollar outlay as the cash buyer, the option buyer could have purchased calls on 400 shares and netted a profit of $2,600 over and above a $1,400 investment.

The best way to analyze the attractiveness of a situation is by estimating the reward/risk potential. If, before entering into the Ampex situation, one had estimated that there was an equal likelihood of APX falling to 6½ as well as advancing to 25, the least risk approach with the best profit opportunity would have been evident. The cash buyer would realize that he was risking a loss of $850 to make a possible $1,000 gain. Thus the reward/risk ratio represents $1,000 divided by $850, or 1.18—a reward only marginally greater than the risk. On the other hand, the option buyer would have been risking $350 for a $650 profit. The reward/risk ratio would be 1.86, or approximately a 2-to-1 chance for gain as opposed to loss.

This very simple reward/risk analysis must be used with the awareness that there is a wide range of stock prices where an option has negative value while a long outright position in the stock might actually show a profit. Figure 1 depicts in greater detail the price mechanics of Ampex in the example cited below.

As can be seen, the call option is a complete loss any time APX common is less than 18½, based on the likely premise that there is no resale market for the option. This price is derived from the strike price of 15 plus the call premium of $350 or 3½ points. The common stock, of course, immediately makes or loses money with any price change away from 15. It doesn't make any difference whether the stock was bought on margin or not if in each case 100 shares are owned. As the common advances from 15, it promptly accrues profit. As soon as the $350 premium money is earned, the call begins to show a profit, earning dollar for dollar with the common stock.

Figure 2 reflects the margin buyer's, cash buyer's, and call buyer's situation by plotting percentage profit and loss versus the APX common price.

Just as in the previous figure, the call buyer is under water until APX hits 18½. At this same point the cash buyer has a 23 percent profit and the margin buyer a 42 percent profit. At about 19½ the call buyer goes ahead of the cash buyer and ahead of the margin buyer at 21. After 21 the call buyer's percentage profit rapidly outstrips the outright stock owners.

On the downside, the call buyer has a 100 percent loss without the stock even dropping. As APX declines, the margin buyer's loss accelerates relative to the cash buyer's for every point drop of the common.

Above all, these illustrations point out that OTC options are attractive only on highly volatile stocks. Small price movements are just as deadly as contrary price movements to the option

FIGURE 1   Profits and Losses at Different APX Prices

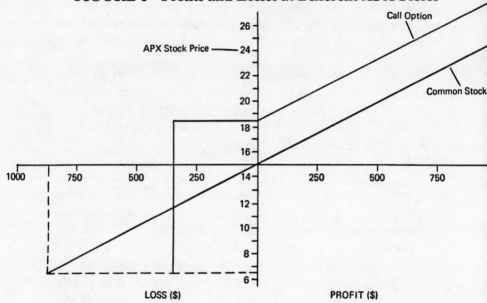

FIGURE 2   Percent Profits and Losses at Different APX Prices

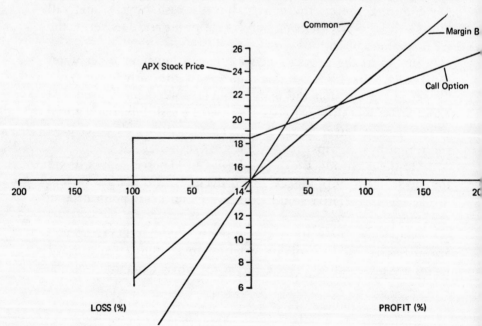

buyer. It takes big swings in prices so that the option holder can first recover the cost of his option and then go on to make a profit.

It might be added that Figure 2 clearly illustrates that holding stocks on margin is a *highly* risky affair. Margined stocks are the most perilous in a falling market and don't profit as well as calls in a rapidly rising market. Interestingly enough, however, a margined stock position *in combination* with options can be a very conservative strategy. This is exactly what Russell Sage espoused. More about this later.

The last examples have used prices, profits, and returns without taking into account commission costs. However, when comparing several approaches for the acquisition of 100 shares of stock, the commission costs will be the same in each case. Nonetheless, this cost has not been ignored because it is negligible. It is not.

A good rule of thumb is to figure a commission cost of 1½ times the price of the underlying stock to either exercise the call or resell the stock. As an example, to exercise a call with a strike price of 45 will cost approximately $67. This charge can be considerably more than the "rule" for very low-priced stocks and somewhat less for high-priced stocks. Nonetheless, it's a fair average. Yet, the best "rule" in these times of changing, negotiated rates is to check with your broker before making the analysis.

Buying Puts

Option buyers are much more enthusiastic about calls than puts. This is reflected in the price. A call normally commands a 20 percent higher premium than a put option on the same stock. Whether this is due to some endemic optimism ingrained in the psyche of the New World, self-righteous indignation toward short selling, or a perverse rejection of economic reality, calls have always been in greater demand than puts. The market for puts seems to be supported by the so-called more sophisticated speculators. If "more sophisticated" can be taken to mean "more realistic," a pretty good case can be made.

On the average, and over the last four decades, every three years of an advancing market have been followed by one year of a declining market. Even though the general trend has been up over the period (who knows from here?), the records substantiate that the drops have usually been about twice as rapid as the advances. While the ideal would be to buy at the bottom and sell out at the top, in practice this seldom occurs, because the speculator tends to wait for confirmation of the trend. By the time certainty seems assured, a preponderance of the general price movement has often already happened. Consequently, in the three-year uptrend, a speculator might be on the right side of the movement no more than half of the time. If he is in the market for one and a half to two years on the upside leg, and is out on the downside in a total four-year cycle, he would be active less than 50 percent of the time! Such a speculator's time would be more profitably spent selling cosmetics door to door.

If one is going to speculate, he's foolish not to use all the tools available to him. One of the most underrated and often ignored tools in the accomplished speculator's kit for operating in a down market is the put option.

A dispassionate analyst of finance recognizes that in a world of chance, the possibility of a loss is really not much less than that of a gain. Managerial intent and hopes have nothing to do with the odds. A capricious government edict, a natural disaster in an overseas marketplace, or the abrupt emergence of a new hostile foreign attitude can turn the market end for end. Be damned with a security's intrinsic value! Intrinsic is only what someone else will pay for the stock. The sooner one disassociates his judgment from his desires, the better able he will be to take full advantage of money-making opportunities.

One speculator, Jeb Wofford, gained a degree of fame by being audacious enough to put his money where his judgment dictated. Early in 1962, Jeb came to the conclusion that the stock market had reached a precariously high level and that both the economy and the market were due for a major correction. He arrived in New York with a reputed $30,000. Studying all the strategies for capitalizing on his bearish projections, he decided that put options would be both the safest and most profitable line of attack.

Wofford's appraisal of an incipient break was right on the nose. Table 4 has been prepared from Elizabeth Fowler's book *Ninety Days to Fortune*. This work also recounts the whole Wofford saga.

TABLE 4

1961 Highs versus 1962 Lows for Selected Stocks

	1961 High	1962 Lows	Percent Loss
IBM	607	300	50
Litton	82⅞	38¼	54
Beckman	159¾	62⅛	61
Texas Instruments	206¾	49	76
Ampex	27¾	10	64
Amp, Inc.	34¼	17	50
NCR	142½	66¾	53
Alberto Culver	60¼	35	42
Revlon	84	31	63
Brunswick	74⅞	13⅛	82
Anken	86¾	28¾	67

The average loss for the above list of "glamors" was 60 percent —a major correction with a vengeance.

Wofford reasoned that regardless of attractive projected earnings for the coming year, the big "high-flyers" would surely be caught in the downdraft of the falling, less seasoned, speculative issues.

On April 16, he bought a put on Xerox at $154 that was due to expire on June 4. This gave him the right to sell 100 shares of Xerox at $154 to the option seller on any day up to June 4. He paid a hefty $1,148, with less than two months of life for the option left. However, on the day he bought the put, Xerox was trading at 145⅜. Consequently, his option was "in-the-money" by 154 less 145⅜, or 8⅝ points. Applied to the 100 shares, this was equivalent to $862.50. In other words, if he had exercised the put on the same day he bought it, he would have received $862.50 less commissions. This is the amount by which the put option he bought was "in-the-money," or already profitable.

The net effect is that Wofford paid $1,148 less the built-in profit of $862.50, or $285.50 for the remaining seven weeks of the option. On an annualized basis, this premium was equivalent to $1,920 for a put on a highly volatile $145 stock. That premium works out to a mere 13 percent a year—a real bargain! On the other hand, Wofford had only seven weeks to show a profit. Additionally, if Xerox recovered and Wofford couldn't find someone else willing to buy the put from him, the full $1,148 was at risk.

Needless to say, Wofford was golden. The gradual slide that had started early in 1962 turned into an avalanche:

XRX

Feb 2	148
March 1	145
April 2	154
April 16	*145⅜*
May 1	144⅜
May 16	131¾
May 28	110¼
June 4	105½

The major one-day break in the 1962 bear market occurred on May 28. This would have been an appealing day to exercise. However, the truism with OTC options is that the premium buys time. So he held to the last day. Then he bought 100 shares of XRX (he didn't catch the day's low and paid 111½) and in turn delivered them to the original option seller at the 154 price.

His profit on the deal was 154 minus 111½ times 100 shares, or, $4,250 gross before the double commission. On a net commission basis, he paid $11,200.15 to buy the 100 **XRX** and received $15,335.44 when he delivered the 100 **XRX**. His net profit was $4,135.29 less his investment of $1,148, or $2,987.29. That's a nifty 260 percent return in seven weeks!

Concurrently with the Xerox operation, he bought puts on U.S. Steel at 72 for $450 each. These options worked out even better.

U.S. Steel (X)

Feb 2	72⅜
Mar. 1	71¼
Apr. 2	70⅜
May 1	59½
May 28	50⅜
June 1	52⅛

A few days after the May 28 break, Wofford exercised his puts by buying the stock at 52⅞ for a net cost of $5,331.70 per 100 and put them to the option seller at 72. He realized $7,121.92 per 100 from the delivery. The difference was $1,790.13. His profit, less the initial investment of $450, was $1,340.13, which amounted to a return on investment of a whopping 298 percent.

Wofford also bought puts on IBM:

IBM

Feb. 1	554
March 1	543
April 2	525
May 1	462
May 28	361
June 1	385
June 14	300

He was reputed to have cleared $63,000 over and above his $30,725 premium cost.

Wofford's foray into put options was reported to have made him a very wealthy man. Complete disclosure of the figures has never been made public. Nonetheless, there can be no doubt that he cleaned up like an army sergeant in a recruits' crap game.

Considering that Wofford acted on his convictions with the courage of a brass monkey and the wisdom of a raving ape, he made out quite well. However, his fortune was secured with the aid of a huge smile from the goddess of luck. He risked all of his capital on his belief that prices would plummet in only a few months. If his judgment had been right but his timing off just a hair, he would have been wiped out. He had to be right on both counts. A more prudent speculator would have worked with a mixed bag of puts, short sales, and short sales hedged with calls. The returns probably would have been less spectacular, but so would have been the risk.

The ironical denouement to the Wofford story is an excellent example of the imprudence of foolhardy audaciousness. Wofford had made a killing, a real sweep, only to be overcome by his most dangerous adversary—himself.

A young, inexperienced man's greatest enemy is himself. The self-satisfaction of the first success engenders a feeling of omni-science. Without an occasional sting from defeat, one's confidence can reach enormous proportions. Wofford took his short side profits and reinvested in calls on gold-producing companies. He reasoned that the gold outflow that accompanied the falling stock market would force a currency devaluation, thereby greatly en-hancing the earnings of the mining companies. Here again Wofford's judgment was correct. Unfortunately, his timing of the impending devaluation was off by more than ten years! The mining stocks did not have a spectacular surge in the fall of 1962. Presumably the calls expired and the capital was lost. Wofford has neither confirmed nor denied whether this is what happened. However, the odds are that his silence has been more likely gloomy than golden.

Straddle Strategy

The combination of the put and the call—the straddle—is particularly attractive in wildly and widely fluctuating markets. Option writers love to write straddles because they receive nearly twice the income they would if they wrote only a single option. (Since a call sells for approximately 20 percent more than a put, the total income from a straddle is divided approximately 55 percent from the call and 45 percent from the put.) Option buyers are attracted to straddles because they can turn a profit no matter which way the market moves—*as long as it moves!* Consequently, the timing of the straddle purchase is much less critical. One needn't be in at the beginning of a major move. A straddle bought near the end of either a bear or bull move can pay off handsomely. Prices both fall and rise dramatically in the last stages of their respective phases so that one can exercise, say, the put side, and subsequently have the call side come "into the money" on the rebound.

A hypothetical example will demonstrate the interesting aspects of straddle strategy.[1] Let's take the case of a stock currently at 30, which had a previous low of 18 and a near term possibility of popping up to 40. The trader who researched the stock has several available strategies. He could buy the stock outright and wait for the stock to hit his upward projection. He could buy 90-day straddles in anticipation that the stock might retest its old low before making its advance. Lastly, he could use a combination of straddles and stock. This latter approach introduces the concept of trading against an option. This most valuable tactic will also be discussed in a subsequent section.

Table 5 is a compilation of the various results of each strategy under varying price assumptions. In all cases, commission costs have been ignored for simplicity.

Let's now examine each approach at each stock price assumption. If the stock were to rise uninterruptedly from 30 to 40 in less

---

1. The example is patterned after one used in a market letter by Marsh, Block, Leibler & Co., Inc., member Put and Call Brokers and Dealers Association, Inc.

TABLE 5

Straddle and Combination Straddle Results

Stock Price	Case 1 Buy 500 Shares @ 500			Case 2 Buy 5 Straddles (600 ea.) @ 30			Case 3 Buy 5 Straddles ($600 ea.) @ 30 Buy 400 Shares @ 25		
	Profit ($)	Invest. ($)	Return (%)	Profit ($)	Invest. ($)	Return (%)	Profit ($)	Invest. ($)	Return (%)
30 to 40	500	15,000	33⅓	2,000	3,000	66⅔	2,000	3,000	66⅔
30 to 25	−2,500	15,000	−16⅔	−500	3,000	−16⅔	−500	13,000	−3.8
30 to 18	−6,000	15,000	−40	3,000	3,000	100	200	13,000	1.5
30 to 25 to 40	5,000	15,000	33⅓	4,500	3,000	150	8,000	13,000	62

than three months, the cash buyer of 500 shares would capture a quick 10-point, or $5,000, profit. Ten points with 5 straddles would also yield the same $5,000, but in this case the cost of the straddles (5 times $600 for each 3-month straddle, or $3,000) would first have to be deducted to leave a net profit of $2,000.

If, on the other hand, the stock sagged to 25, the cash buyer would show a loss on his 500 shares of $2,500. The straddle holder would have a cash value of $2,500 on his puts, $500 short of covering the $3,000 cost.

A shrewd straddle trader could, at this point, buy 400 shares of stock at 25 for a total additional investment of $10,000 over and above his original $3,000 (Case 3). The logic of this move will unfold in the coming analysis.

If the sag continued until the stock returned to its old low of 18, the cash buyer would now be out $6,000. The straightforward straddle buyer would, if the stock stayed at 18 until expiration, show a $3,000 profit from his puts over and above his cost. The straddle trader would also show a modest profit. First, he would put his 400 shares bought at 25 to the straddle seller at 30 for a $2,000 gross profit. Then, he would exercise the fifth straddle by buying the 100 shares of stock at 18 and putting them at 30 for a $1,200 return. The total receipts of $3,200 would cover his straddle outlay of $3,000 with a modest $200 net profit on the overall transaction. The essence of the straddle trader's strategy was that he bought his 400 shares with no risk of any real loss whatsoever.

The final hypothesized price history represents an equally probable pattern of events. J. P. Morgan was once asked to characterize the stock market. His simple answer, based on a lifetime of observation and experience, was "It will fluctuate." A newly bought stock seldom takes off immediately. One can expect a period of backing and filling. If the original premise for the purchase was justified, the stock will eventually reach the target.

Let us now presume that the stock moved from 30 down to 25 and then back up to 40. The cash buyer, by holding tight and sweating it out, finally would reap his $5,000 profit. Of course, if he had sold out at 25 and not bought back in at 18, he would have had a respectable loss.

The straddle buyer who exercised at 25 would have had a $500 loss at the time, but he would have recouped $2,500 of his original option cost. Then, when the stock rebounded to 40, his 5 unexercised calls would have generated $5,000 for a total net profit of $4,500.

The straddle trader would have made out like a bandit. Having bought 400 shares at 25, he was more than fully protected if the price moved lower. When the price recovered to 40, he would have had a 15-point profit in the stock, or $6,000—*plus,* he could exercise his 5 calls at 30 for an additional $2,000 profit over his $3,000 cost: a grand total profit of $8,000.

The percent return column in Table 6 for the three cases clearly depicts the benefits and risks of each approach. Over the postulated price ranges, the cash buyer of stock was almost constantly at risk while both the straddle buyer and straddle trader were relatively immune. At the very worst, both the straddle buyer and straddle trader would have lost their $3,000 premium if the stock hadn't moved.

However, sticking with the scenarios, let's now briefly examine the reward/risk ratios over the entire range of postulated price movements.

TABLE 6
Straddle and Combination Straddle Reward/Risk Ratio

	Case 1		Case 2		Case 3	
	$	%	$	%	$	%
Maximum Loss	6,000	−40	500	−16⅔	500	−3.8
Maximum Gain	5,000	33⅓	4,500	150	8,000	62
Reward/ Risk		.83	.83	9	9	16	16

If at the onset there was an equal probability that the price changes used in Table 5 would occur, the reward/risk ratios shown in Table 6 definitely point out the only intelligent way to get involved. In a wildly swinging market, where long-term fundamentals can be expected to have little or no impact, an outright long (or even short) position is foolishness. The straddle as depicted in Case 2 has the obvious advantage of virtually unlimited gain with very limited risk. The more sophisticated use of straddles combined with common stock (Case 3) offers a significant improvement in potential gain. The secret to the success of the Case 3 strategy is that the additional capital in the form of 400 shares bought at 25 is infused at a point where there can be no loss if the price continues down (in fact there will be a profit from the fifth put), and an unrestricted gain from an upward bounce.

Option Hedging

While speculators predominate as option buyers, there are a number of investors who also use options for more conservative purposes. Options offer a unique latitude of investment decision. They allow the holder to make a revocable decision, which he can choose at some later time either to stand by or not. Options, because of their limited cost exposure, can also be used as insurance for other investment situations. Just as with an insurance policy, one isn't disappointed that, having paid the premium, he doesn't receive the insurance money. However, there are instances in which one can collect on the policy without figuratively having to die.

There are thousands of different institutions that participate in the stock market. There are banks, pension funds, life insurance companies, etc. Regardless of their disparate principal activities, one characteristic is common to all. Day after day new funds flow into their coffers to be invested. If they don't have a certain amount of money on hand at one particular moment, they pretty much know when it will come in. These institutions, as well as some wealthy individual investors, sometimes buy calls on a stock that they feel is attractively situated in anticipation of owning the stock via the option when the option expires. In this manner they can take advantage of an immediate situation without having the full amount of capital required for the investment. In the truest sense, they have bought time with their option money. Of course, if their judgment was erroneous and the stock declined sharply, they would have lost only the relatively small option premium; the much larger portion of capital would have been preserved for some more worthwhile purchase.

The most fascinating and varied reason for buying options —both puts and calls—is for insurance. This approach is usually referred to as hedging. One can hedge after a profit has been secured or in anticipation of making a profit. Hedging can also be an effective tool to prevent further losses as well as to create an opportunity to recoup losses.

Options are used to "lock in" the profit in a situation when some uncertainty arises that leads one to reappraise his position. This is the insurance approach. Let us take the case of an investor who bought 100 shares of Control Data at 34 in 1970. Just the previous year Control Data had been selling for as high as 150 and the $34 tab seemed to discount every disaster short of bankruptcy. Within months CD barrelled up to 55 on the wings of the buoyant recovery market of late 1970-early 1971.

Alert market observers are aware that any abrupt market movement, regardless of direction, always accumulates the elements of a correction along the way. This action, almost always technical in nature, happens regardless of the fundamentals of the stock. In an uptrend, the buyers will suddenly take their profits; in a down move they will cover shorts. Sometimes this correction is mild, other times quite sharp. Usually the severity of the correction is a direct function of the rapidity of the initial move.

The investor had three choices at this juncture. Recognizing that CD might go still higher, he could simply hold on and hope that he could get out at some level higher than 55 before a sell-off struck. Secondly, he could sell out at 55, take $2,100 gross profit, pay his taxes, and let someone else reap any further rewards as well as the risk. Lastly, he could hedge with a put.

In the early spring of 1971, a six-month-and-ten-day put on CD at 55 could be bought for about $600. The cost of the put premium would come out of the already accumulated paper profit. The put would be a short-term insurance policy. In no case could the investor lose the remaining $2,100 minus $600, or $1,500 profit. If CD collapsed the day after the put was bought, the investor could put his 100 shares to the put seller at 55 and collect his $1,500 profit. On the other hand, the investor did not abandon the possibility of further profit. If CD kept going up, he could let the put expire and sell his stock at the higher price.

As fate would have it, within three months Control Data hit 84. At this point the paper profit was 84 minus 34 times 100, or $5,000, less the cost of $600 of the put at 55. Here again the investor would have faced the same alternatives as before, except that the cost of another put would be somewhat higher because of the higher stock price. At 84, the price of a six-month-and-ten-day put would probably be up to $800. If the investor were to follow a consistent pattern of hedging, he would periodically plow back a portion of his profits into protective puts just to make sure he could nail down the larger portion of profit, come what may. At the same time he is accumulating a short position via the put options, which could in their own right turn a profit.

Within three months CD fell back to 55 and, in another three months, all the way back down to the 34 starting price. If the investor had not hedged, he would have lost his whole paper profit. The hedging investor would have "locked in" a substantial portion of his paper profit. The first put bought at 55 would have been valueless when the stock rose to 84 in the first three months and then declined to the strike price of 55 in the next three months. However, the second put bought at 84 could have been exercised at 34 for a gross return of $5,000. Subtracting the $600 paid for the first put and $800 for the second, the profit from the option hedge would have been $3,600. If the investor had been lucky or perspicacious enough to sell his stock at the top, he would have added another $5,000 to his bank account.

This same hedge works equally well to protect profits accrued from selling short a vulnerable stock. In the short hedge, the short seller with a gain would buy a call or a mix of calls, which would assure him a source of cheap stock to cover his short position if the stock sold short were suddenly to reverse itself and advance.

The story has been told of an intriguing hedge that Jesse Livermore once devised. One of the most celebrated manipulators of his time, Livermore used options extensively in his stock operations. Coming onto the scene in the early part of the twentieth century, he had been a great student of Sage's and had studied his machinations well.

Livermore had been approached by a syndicate of business-men who wanted to distribute to the public their 70 percent hold-ings of a large steel company. Not only did they want to peddle the stock, they also wanted it sold at prices quite a bit above the going rate. Although Livermore was fascinated by the challenge of the magnitude of the deal, he had some reservations about the integrity of the insiders. If any portion of their gigantic holdings came to the marketplace while he was creating a demand for the stock, he feared that both he and the public would wind up with a satchel full of stock at distress prices. Thus, while he requested and received calls on 100,000 shares at prices ranging from 70 to 100, Livermore made one further demand. He insisted that the syndicate deposit all their shares under an iron-clad trust agree-ment, which he alone administered. With one swoop, he locked up 70 percent of the potential sellers, protected himself from any over-eager sandbaggers, and virtually guaranteed the profitability of his options. One would be hard pressed to imagine a more effective hedge against the vicissitudes of either man or fortune.

The second purpose for the calls was to assure his profit. Interestingly enough, Livermore used his calls primarily as a trading vehicle and took the bulk of his profit from short sales, not the calls themselves.

Once the calls were sewed up, Livermore commenced the manipulation. First, he would start buying the stock outright to create activity. Normally he would test the market by buying a few good chunks and observing the resulting price movement. In this way he could get the feel for how much buying it would take to move the stock up a given number of points. Simultaneously, he would let out the word that certain big interests were going to "take the stock in hand." As the stock began to move, the traders, and then the public, would pick up the action and begin to buy. If his campaign succeeded and the price continued up without any more help from Livermore, he would gradually sell out all the stock acquired initially and then continue to sell short. Since he was long the original calls, the short sale of the rising stock was fully insured.

At some point or another, the stock would finally falter. When reaction set in and the stock started down, he would cover his shorts. The purpose was to demonstrate that there was a good demand for the stock even at falling prices. He never wanted one of his manipulations to look like a one-shot deal. This supporting action he called the "stabilizing process." As the stock recovered, he would begin again to sell short on the rise so that he could begin the stabilizing process again when required. Livermore was a clear master of the most judicious and profitable deployment of options for insurance.

While options can be used to "lock in" profits, as a variation they can also be used to salvage a potentially disastrous investment situation.

As has already been said, option writers tend to be wealthy, conservative institutions or individuals. However, such attributes don't exempt them from financial misfortune. Consequently, sagacious option writers tend to be more knowledgeable than most about the advantages and proper use of options.

A good friend of mine has been an active option writer for years. When I say option writer, I mean only that this has been his principal orientation, but certainly not to the exclusion of option buying. When he first cut his teeth in the field, he rapidly came to recognize that flexibility was absolutely vital to success. The example he has given to me is an unusually apt demonstration of the intelligent use of options.

Early in 1973, he bought 200 shares of Syntex at 80 with the idea of writing calls against the stock at about the $90 level. This plan went awry when Syntex (SYN) promptly slumped to the mid-60s and gave every indication of going lower. At this point, my friend reassessed his ideas and came up with the following conclusions:

1. Writing calls against a rapidly falling stock held long is a very poor hedge unless one has no other alternative.

2. Syntex was a good stock and would probably come back at some time in the future.

3. It would be foolish to pump more blood into a failing patient.

4. He was an investor who did not have the stomach to sit tight and take what could be a grievous short-term loss.

From these conclusions he developed the following attack:

1. Sell off half his stock, 100 shares. When originally purchased at 80, the 200 shares of SYN had cost $16,105, including commissions. This was equivalent to $8,052.50 per 100. He sold 100 shares of SYN at 68¾, which netted him $6,834. He had locked in a real loss of $1,218.50 with an equivalent paper loss on the books for the remaining 100 shares.

2. From the proceeds of the sale, he bought an "in-the-money" straddle on SYN at 81½, which had been offered to him for $1,530. The straddle still had

four months left to run. The original investment of $16,105 had been reduced by $6,834 from the sale of the 100 shares and increased by $1,530 for the cost of the straddle. The new investment was $10,801 and this was almost fully protected from any further diminution by the straddle.

Just as he had feared, SYN completely fell out of bed on the news of lowered projected earnings for the end of 1973. Within two months, the stock reached 50½. At this point he judged that the worst was definitely over for SYN because the market had overly discounted a temporary, minor reduction in earnings. Consequently, he exercised the put side of the straddle. He bought 100 SYN at 50½ for a net cost of $5,098 and put them at 81½ for a return of $8,095. His profit on exercising was $8,095 less $5,098, or $2,997. This profit further reduced his investment of $10,801 to $7,804. For this remaining investment he was long 100 shares of SYN with a market price of 50½ and still held one call with a strike price 30 points over the market. The probability that the stock would appreciate from 50½ was quite good, while the likelihood of the calls ever having any value was pretty remote.

Here again, his judgment was impeccable. Within the next two months, SYN dropped farther to its low for the year of 46¼ and then leaped upwards to 90¼ on news of FDA approval of a major new Syntex drug. As the call portion of the straddle neared expiration, he exercised by calling 100 shares at 81½ for a cost of $8,220 and sold the same shares in the open market for $8,935. The profit on the exercise was $715. He also sold the 100 shares he had held through the whole ordeal for another $8,935. Since his investment up to this point was $7,804, he actually recouped all his capital and made an overall profit of $1,846.

Table 7 recaps the whole train of transactions.

The way the whole episode was handled reflected one man's judgment. Naturally there were several other possibilities. At each step a decision was made which would have altered the outcome substantially if some other choice had been decided upon. Reviewing the alternatives might shed some light on the thinking of an experienced investor and option user.

TABLE 7

Recap of Syntex Hedge

(All numbers in dollars)

			Profit/Loss
1. Bot 200 SYN @ 80		16,105	
Investment	16,105		
2. Bot 1 Straddle @ 81½		1,530	
Sold 100 SYN @ 68¾			6,834
Investment	10,801		(1,218)
3. Exercise put			
Bot 100 SYN @ 50½		5,098	
Put 100 SYN @ 81½			8,095
Investment	7,804		2,997
4. Exercise call			
Called 100 SYN @ 81½		8,220	
Sold 100 SYN @ 90¼			8,935
Investment	7,089		715
5. Sold 100 SYN @ 90¼			8,935
Total profit	1,846		

The first, most obvious choice would have been to hold on to all 200 shares of Syntex and ride the storm out. This would have been a difficult choice when all the signs looked like SYN was going lower. Yet an investor with guts could have watched SYN plunge from 80 to 46¼, a 42 percent depreciation, and still have come out quite well.

Bot 200 SYN @ 80	$16,105	
Sold 200 SYN @ 90¼		$17,870
Profit		$1,765

One comment. Syntex recovered. If this buy-and-hold tactic had been used during the same period with a high quality stock such as Ford, the results would have been dismal. Both Syntex and Ford were at 80 in early 1973. By the end of 1973, SYN passed 90¼ and settled around 112. Ford, on the other hand, plunged to a low of 38 and closed out the year at 42. There is a distinct possibility that Ford might stay at the 40 level for years to come.

The next decision point was the sale of 100 shares and the purchase of the in-the-money straddle with part of the proceeds. The other alternative would have been to sell out all 200 shares and take the loss.

Bot 200 SYN @ 80	$16,105	
Sold 200 SYN @ 68¾		$13,688
Loss		($2,437)

This would free all the capital for investment in some other prospect that might be more profitable. However, by selling off only half the shares and buying the straddle to get downside insurance for the remaining 100 shares, the decision was made that SYN was a fundamentally sound investment despite the short-term price weakness.

The last decision point was reached when the put side of the straddle was exercised for a profit, thereby leaving the 100 shares of SYN exposed to further possible downside risk. As opposed to exercising, he could have put the 100 shares he was long rather than buying 100 shares in the market and putting them. As long as there was any life left in the straddle and the price of SYN was below 81½, the 100-share portion of the original position could be put at the strike price of 81½.

Previous Investment $10,801
Put 100 shares @ 81½ $8,095
    Loss   ($2,706)

    This would have finally established the total loss on the Syntex stock. The only hope for recovery would come from any residual value from the call side of the straddle. As it turned out, the modest return of $715 from exercising the call side would have reduced the total loss to $2,706 less $715, or $1,991. By exercising the put by buying new shares in the market and holding on to the old 100 shares, the decision was made that Syntex with a lower average price was much less risky than SYN at 80. In retrospect, this was the correct decision. It should be acknowledged, however, that had Syntex performed like Ford, lifting the hedge by exercising the put would have made some short-term money, but the ultimate loss on the 100 shares exposed could have been incalculably larger.

TABLE 8

Summary of Syntex Alternatives

(All numbers in dollars)

			Profit/Loss
1. Buy and hold			
Bot 200 SYN @ 80	16,105		
Sold 200 SYN @ 90¼		17,870	1,765
2. Hedge, exercise put exercise call, sell stock (Table 7)			1,846
3. Sell out on first drop			
Bot 200 SYN @ 80	16,105		
Sold 200 SYN @ 68¾		13,668	(2,437)
4. Hedge, put 100 shares, exercise call.			(1,991)

Table 8 summarizes the most obvious alternatives to the strategy used by my friend. Regardless of the variation in the performance at the different decision levels, the most notable conclusion that can be drawn is that option hedging can be an extremely valuable tool, not only for protection, but even for turning around an unsatisfactory position.

The results from the basic hedge strategy and all the hedge variations would have been somewhat different if my friend had been able to buy a new straddle, instead of an old in-the-money straddle. This is one of the disadvantages of the OTC market. Just when you want a certain option, there might not be a willing seller around. The option dealers would like their customers to believe that the market is nearly continuous, but in practice there are oftentimes gaping holes. The cost of the in-the-money straddle was greater than a new straddle by the amount of profit in it at the time of its sale adjusted for the partly elapsed option duration. If a new unconventional four-month straddle on SYN could have been bought when needed, it would have cost about $925, or more than $600 less than the in-the-money straddle that had to be used for hedging. Nonetheless, this kind of difficulty should never deter a conservative investor from option hedging. A little inconvenience is well worth the protection afforded by the intelligent use of options.

One final historical example will demonstrate the long-standing versatility of options, particularly in financial maneuvers requiring a deft touch. In the early months of 1884, Jay Gould, one of the most flamboyant and feared of the railroad "barons" of that age, decided to make a move to extend his Wabash Railroad to the eastern seaboard. His plan was to pry control of the Lake Shore Railroad from the tight grasp of the Vanderbilts and then move on to the Erie or the New York Central to complete the link. During the early months of that year, Gould began buying every share of the Lake Shore that was offered for sale.

Needless to say, "Uncle" Russell Sage played the role of the bagman for the whole deal. He lent Gould the money (at interest) with which to mount the raid. While not using the conversion ploy, Sage nonetheless extracted from Gould thousands of puts on the Lake Shore stock as a condition of lending him the money. In addition, the stock Gould bought was also to be the collateral for the loan. If Gould's raid were successful and the price of Lake Shore stock were to rise, Sage's collateral would be safe. If Gould's manipulation failed and there was any subsequent drop in the price of the stock, Sage could buy the cheaper stock in the market and put it to Gould at the higher option price. The profits from the puts would offset any loss of value in the collateralized stock. Consequently, Sage's capital was safe, with Gould bearing all the risk. For his part, Gould would get a nearly free ride (excepting interest costs)—if he were successful. He had all of Sage's money behind him to guarantee a victory.

In this particular instance, Sage couldn't resist the temptation to make a little extra profit over and above the interest on his loan. He sold puts on Lake Shore stock at retail for handsome premiums. The speculating public eagerly bought the puts because they were convinced that no one, not even Gould, could conquer the Vanderbilts. The puts that Sage sold were in turn backed by Gould's free puts. If the common stock price rose, the puts would expire and Sage could keep the premium from the puts as an extra profit. If the common dropped and the stock was put to him, Sage could in turn put it to Gould at no cost to himself. The premium he received from selling the puts was his insurance against the drop in value of the collateralized stock.

In May 1884, the brokerage firm of Grant and Ward unexpectedly failed. The company was a partnership consisting of General Ulysses S. Grant's son and an opportunistic scoundrel as general partners, with the general himself as a limited partner. The failure caused what has since been dubbed the "rich man's panic."

Prices of the leading railroad shares broke sharply, with Lake Shore leading the parade. Since it had been rumored that Sage had sold thousands of puts on the stock and might not be able to honor such staggering commitments, his office was deluged with clients who wanted to put their stock to him. At first, Sage stalled and bickered. He opened his office late and closed early. It was almost as if he enjoyed jousting with the rapacious pack. Nevertheless, he paid out over $7,000,000 in three days' time. By meeting his obligations, Sage's reputation and subsequent business volume were greatly enhanced. Of course, it was not until many years later that anyone realized that Sage had not lost a cent and that the whole cost had perforce been swallowed by Jay Gould.

So far we've seen options used to lock in a profit, and insure against further loss. Puts and calls can also be incorporated into a straight option hedge wherein the option and related common position are established simultaneously. The option hedge should be used whenever one is dealing with a stock noted for its high volatility. In recent years, there have been hardly any stocks, including the most precious blue chips, which haven't turned out to be more reactive than expected. If one is using margin, the option hedge is an indispensable defensive tool.

Special attention should be given to the option hedge, particularly when selling short a common stock. In this instance a protective call is bought at the same time the stock is shorted. Consequently, both the short sale and option strike price would be affected at essentially the same price. If the stock unexpectedly advances, stock can be called away at the option strike price to replace the borrowed stock without having to chase a runaway stock. Actually this option protection costs more than if one were buying stock with a concomitant protective put because calls cost more than puts. However, a short sale needs more protection, not necessarily because of any greater inherent risk, but because short sellers themselves seem to be more nervous.

The cost of the option is an insurance policy against being wrong. Years ago a ballroom dancer wrote a book about making a million dollars by using stops whenever a stock was bought or sold short. If he were to buy a stock at 30, he would place a sell stop order with his broker somewhat below the market, say at 27. If the stock were to back off from 30 and then actually trade at 27, the stop would be activated and the stock sold at the market. In a rapidly falling market, the stock might actually be sold several points below the stop price. Normally, however, the sale would take place fairly near the stop.

If the same stock were sold short at 30, a buy stop would be placed above the market, say at 32. The logic behind this approach is to get out of a bad situation before it gets worse. The whole process is completely automatic and requires no attention. If one tends to ignore his holdings, or for one reason or another cannot keep close tabs on them, stops can protect a position from catastrophic loss. On the other hand, one disadvantage is that a perfectly satisfactory position can be liquidated by a brief, aberrant swing of the market. Another is that the presence of a large number of stop orders in the market can actually cause wide swings, which will in turn trigger more stops.

The use of an option instead of a stop can often better serve the same purpose. Seldom would a stop be placed within 10 percent of the current price of the stock. Otherwise it is likely to be accidentally set off. Normally a 90-day put or call can be bought for 10 percent or less of the cost of the stock. Consequently, the option provides the same protection for the same or slightly less cost exposure, but with far greater flexibility. The option is exercised by choice, not automatically and blindly.

Throughout this chapter several instances have been given of using combinations of options and the related stock. An option trader will use the common stock to lock in a profit and at the same time avail himself of a trading medium. If a put buyer who paid $350 for a 90-day put at 40 finds the stock at 30 in one month and exercises, he will receive his $1,000 less $350, or $650 as profit. However, he would be giving up two months of the option's life when he exercises. He can accomplish the same purpose, but leave his choices open, by simply buying 100 shares but not putting them. If the stock were to rise 10 points in the next month and then start to turn weak again, the put owner would sell his 100 shares, take his profit, and still have one month of life left on his put. Were the stock to drop again, he could finally exercise his put option for another profit.

A stock hedger, who is primarily an investor and not an option trader, reverses the process. His first attention is directed toward the common stock. He then uses the option as insurance, for locking in profit, or for recouping losses.

Options themselves are a very straightforward concept. They offer limited risk and great flexibility. This flexibility seems to pose a big bugaboo when it comes to comprehending all the practical applications of options. Like salt and pepper, they can be used in many combinations in a variety of dishes. Also like the proper seasoning, they can make all the difference in the world between a success or a failure. If an investor or a speculator truly wants to operate on his skill rather than just luck, he must perforce come to grips with the myriad facets of options.

3

The Chicago Board
Options Exchange

As has been repeatedly pointed out in the previous chapter, one of the most serious disadvantages (from the buyer's standpoint) of OTC options is the virtual absence of a resale market. If a man holds an option that has become profitable but that still has considerable life remaining, his two alternatives are either to exercise the option or to lock in the profit by trading against the option. In either instance, the option holder must come up with additional cash to finance the operation and must also pay substantial commission costs based on the higher price of the underlying shares. It is only infrequently that he can just sell his profitable option outright to capture profit with no further financial outlay.

By the same token, an *unprofitable* option with substantial life still remaining can seldom be unloaded to another buyer. The premium paid for the option is valueless to anyone other than the original buyer. Buying OTC options is a great deal like some of the "one-decision" stocks that many of the large institutions have bought themselves into. Once you've got it, you're stuck with it unless it makes money. Their holdings are so large that they can only sell into a rising market. In a dull or down market, there are simply no buyers for a major block. There's no way to cut a loss.

On the other hand, the option writer has much more latitude. If he sold a call against a stock he owns and the stock heads south, he can sell the stock and go "naked." While he must leave margin money in his account to secure the still-outstanding call, with the stock dropping, the call will most likely expire unexercised. If the option writer writes a put against an existing short sale and the price advances, he can likewise cover his short and use cash to secure the outstanding, potentially worthless put. In these ways, writers can more readily limit losses and safeguard their capital.

What this boils down to is that, historically, the option market has been biased for the writer and loaded against the buyer. The odds favor a seller writing against a diversified portfolio. A buyer really needs uncommon skill, luck, and timing to hit enough jackpots to pay off the myriad of complete losses and return a profit. Wofford did it. So have a few others. But history shows that very few men acquired their wealth through buying conventional options. Sage made more money selling options to Gould than Gould made with the options he bought.

Fundamentals of CBOE Options

And then along came the Chicago Board Options Exchange. Conceived by the Chicago Board of Trade (the world's largest commodities futures exchange) in 1969, approved by the SEC in February 1973 for a "pilot operation," the CBOE began trading on April 26, 1973, in call options on sixteen carefully selected stocks. On that day, 911 option contracts exchanged hands. Less than nine months later more than 15,000 contracts per day were trading. The CBOE has clearly stolen the OTC option market's thunder.

Investors and speculators alike had many misgivings about the CBOE before it opened its doors. The multiple and fixed exercise prices, and the fixed expiration dates four times a year were thought to be too confusing. Trading in call options alone (trading in puts might be allowed at a later date) was considered to be too one-sided to be practical, especially when options on only twenty-three stocks would be available. Additionally, many skeptics disdained any association of the new options market with the giant, old commodities market. They apparently felt that the institutional clients who are most often option writers either would not or could not participate in a venture so related.

Admitting that the ultimate viability of the CBOE is not positively assured—the SEC started an evaluation of the "experiment" in late 1973—nonetheless the gloomsayers seem to have been driven from the field. The volume and open interest on the exchange have grown to such an extent that the trading facilities were jam-packed only eight months after the doors were opened. The phenomenal acceptance of this new market stems from a need very capably satisfied.

The CBOE call options were designed for one prime objective— marketability. To achieve this quality, the expiration dates and strike prices on the options have been standardized. Neither changes as the price of the common fluctuates or as time passes. The CBOE, by standardizing all the salient option terms save the price, established the basis for liquidity. The ability to buy, sell, or resell in a public auction has opened a whole new financial realm. An option bought one day can be sold the next, or the day after, or any day up until the expiration date. The prices of the options, the trading volume, and open interest are quoted every day in the *Wall Street Journal*. Instantaneous prices are available during the trading hours from any broker. Not only is the CBOE a resale market for options, it is a public market. The sophisticated and unsophisticated, the professional and the amateur, the wise and the foolish may all participate.

All options traded, regardless of the stock on which the option is a call, have four expiration dates. These are the last trading dates of January, April, July, and October. On any given day, calls with three expiration dates are available. As each option expires, a new one is added. When the January option expires, the October option is added. When April expires, the January option is added. The shortest option that can be bought is one bought on the day it expires. The longest option that can be bought is for nine months. Of course, just before an option month expires, the longest option available is one for six months.

TABLE 9

Comparison of Northwest Airline and Pennzoil CBOE Options

(Prices from close of October 1, 1973)

	Stock Price	Strike Price	October	January	April
Nw A	$26\frac{5}{8}$	30	$\frac{5}{8}$	$2\frac{1}{8}$	unavailable
	$26\frac{5}{8}$	25	$2\frac{3}{8}$	$4\frac{1}{4}$	$5\frac{3}{8}$
	$26\frac{5}{8}$	20	$6\frac{3}{8}$	$7\frac{5}{8}$	$8\frac{1}{4}$
Pennz	$23\frac{7}{8}$	25	$1\frac{1}{16}$	$2\frac{3}{8}$	3
	$23\frac{7}{8}$	20	$3\frac{3}{4}$	$4\frac{7}{8}$	$5\frac{3}{4}$

Table 9 illustrates the salient aspects of the CBOE market with options on two stocks, Northwest Airlines and Pennzoil. As can be seen, on October 1, 1973, there were three option periods available. The October option was good for 30 days, the January for 4 months, and the April for 7 months. One month later, when the October options expired, the January would be good for 3 months, the April for 6 months, and the newly instituted July for 9 months.

Next, it can be seen that each stock has options available with several strike prices. From time to time as the stock price moves away from the existing strike price series, a new strike price series will be introduced by the Exchange. However, as can be seen in Table 9, a new strike price series might not have options created for every option period. The purpose of adding new strike price series is to have a strike price near the price of the underlying stock so that cheap options will always be available.

Just as with the OTC options, CBOE prices are quoted in points. The price of the Nw A Jan 30 is 2⅛. This price is equivalent to $212.50. The Pennz April 20 is 5¾, or $575.

In the OTC market, the cost of a new option is called "the premium" because the strike price is almost always the current market price of the stock under option. Thus the premium is a pure cost charged for the use of the time specified by the option, since the option initially has no intrinsic value. However, on the CBOE, what one pays for an option may be all premium, or no premium at all, or anywhere in between. As an instance, both the Nw A 30 and Pennz 25 options have strike prices higher than the common stock prices. Consequently, the prices of the options are all premium since calls on a stock are worthless when the stock can be bought more cheaply on the open market. The calls have no intrinsic value.

On the other hand, both the Nw A Oct 20 and Pennz Oct 20 options have no premium at all. Taking the Nw A Oct 20 as an example, by paying 6⅜ points one could buy Nw A at 20 for a total cost of 26⅜. With the price of the stock at 26⅝, this January option is actually at a slight discount to its intrinsic value. This discount reflects the transaction costs associated with buying the stock if the option were exercised. The net upshot is that both the Nw A Oct 20 and Pennz Oct 20 are selling at their intrinsic value with no associated premium, for all practical purposes.

The premium that one will pay for an option is a function of the estimated profit potential over the life of the option, factored by the amount of risk. The further the option is in-the-money, the greater is the intrinsic value. The greater the intrinsic value, the greater the cost, and consequently the greater the risk of loss. This is why the more expensive options with a common expiration date will have the lesser premium.

On the other side of the coin, all options are good only for a limited period of time. The longer the option has to run, the more time there is for the option to turn a profit. Table 10 demonstrates that for a given exercise price the premium increases with each longer exercise period.

As one might expect, all premium rapidly disappears as the option approaches its expiration date. Table 11, which shows the Northwest Airlines option prices some three weeks later than those in Table 10, demonstrates this point. The two October options with some intrinsic value are selling at or slightly below that intrinsic value, again reflecting the commission costs.

However, an interesting ambiguity can also be seen by comparing Table 10 with Table 11. The percent premium for the deferred options has actually risen a bit even though the stock price has declined slightly and the life of these options is three weeks less. The most inexorable law of an option is that as it approaches expiration its price will fall to its intrinsic value. If there is no intrinsic value, the price will fall to a nominal amount. Yet, the more deferred options are more free from this pressure and can respond to the individual expectations of each stock for the balance of the option's life.

Trading Options Long Term

Since CBOE call options never run longer than 9 months, buying options is much more akin to trading than to investing. There are no really long-term aspects to options other than the fact that one can take a long-term capital gain on an option held longer than six months. Other than this one longish feature, the option

TABLE 10

Percent Premium of Northwest Airline CBOE Options

(Prices from close of October 1, 1973)

Stock Price	Strike Price	Intrinsic Value	October Price	October Premium		January Price	January Premium		April Price	April Premium	
			$	$	%	$	$	%	$	$	%
26⅝	30	0	⅝	⅝	100	2⅛	2⅛	100	—	—	—
26⅝	25	1⅝	2⅜	¾	31	4¼	2⅝	62	5⅜	3¾	70
26⅝	20	6⅝	6⅜	0	0	7⅝	1	13	8¼	1⅝	20

TABLE 11

Percent Premium of Northwest Airline CBOE Options

(Prices from close of October 25, 1973)

Stock	Strike	Intrinsic Value	October Price	October Premium		January Price	January Premium		April Price	April Premium	
			$	$	%	$	$	%	$	$	%
26¼	30	0	1/16	1/16	100	2¼	2¼	100	—	—	—
26¼	25	1¼	13/16	0	0	4⅜	3⅛	71	5¾	4¼	78
26¼	20	6¼	6⅛	0	0	7⅝	1⅜	18	(a)		

(a) not traded that day

is not an instrument that can be bought and socked away in a safety deposit box.

Nonetheless, there is a difference between long-term and short-term trading. If one buys a call and keeps an occasional eye on the stock price in the evening paper, he is trading long term. He is waiting for the relatively long-term appreciation of the stock and the associated option. Conversely, if he watches the daily prices in the *Wall Street Journal* and is interested in trading out at a profit and then re-entering the market at some other price on a different option, he is a short-term trader. Each approach warrants individual attention.

The long-term CBOE option trader tends to make his purchase with the same approach he would use if he were bidding for a conventional OTC option. In determining whether an option price is attractive, the buyer will make a judgment relating option cost to length of life. Of course, this process pertains only to a rational option buyer, not to one who is stampeded by his optimism to buy anything that moves. In the OTC market, the decision is quite simple since the alternatives are few. On the CBOE, where several strike prices and expiration dates are often traded on the same underlying stock, the decision involves more consideration.

Table 12 is a repeat of the price structure for Northwest Airlines options that was used in an earlier illustration.

TABLE 12

Northwest Airline CBOE Option Prices on Oct. 1, 1973

(Common price @ 26⅝)

Strike Price	Oct (1 mo. life)	Jan (4 mo. life)	April (7 mo. life)
30	⅝	2⅛	—
25	2⅜	4¼	5⅜
20	6⅜	7⅝	8¼

Since the numbers can be arranged and analyzed any number of ways, let's go through a reward/risk study such as the one used in the previous chapter. Obviously a trader would buy a call on Nw A only because he thought the stock was going to advance. (The hedger who thought the stock weak might buy a call to hedge a short sale in the common.) In his own mind he would have an expected target price of 10 percent, 20 percent, or maybe a 50-percent spurt in the common. A 10-percent advance would move the common from 26⅝ to 29¼; 20 percent, from 26⅝ to 32; 50 percent, from 26⅝ to 40.

Table 13 compares the original purchase cost of each Nw A option with the price of the option at its expiration at each assumed level of price advance. The risk is the initial cost of the option and the reward is the price at expiration, since a long-term trader will almost always wait to the very end to get the most time out of the option.

Several observations can be made from the analysis. For the nearby options, the reward/risk ratio dictates that the most attractive option is the one nearest the common stock price if the common makes a moderate upward move. Thus, the October 25 is clearly better than any other if the stock moves up 10 percent and continues to hold its own until the common has advanced nearly 20 percent. As the stock advances further, the reward/risk ratio indicates that the most attractive nearby option would have been the cheapest one—the October 30. This shifting leverage as the stock price advances will be discussed later on.

The more deferred options exhibit similar characteristics, except that the cheapest option doesn't prove to be the most rewarding until after the stock has had a pretty hefty advance.

If one were to make a sweeping generalization, the best option to buy, predicated on a vigorous price rise, is the cheapest one. The more conservative purchaser would select the option with a strike price closest to the stock price.

While the reward/risk analysis is useful, it doesn't provide much insight into what can be expected if the price rise isn't as

TABLE 13

Reward/Risk Analysis for Northwest Airline Options

(Initial common price @ 26⅝)

Common Increase	Strike Prices	October 1 Month Left			January 4 Months Left			April 7 Months Left		
		Risk (Option Cost)	Reward (Expir. Price)	Reward/ Risk Ratio	Risk	Reward	Reward/ Risk Ratio	Risk	Reward	Reward/ Risk Ratio
10% (29¼)	30	⅝	nom.	0	2⅛	nom.	0	—	—	—
	25	2⅜	4¼	1.7	4¼	4¼	1.0	5⅜	4¼	0.8
	20	6⅜	9¼	1.4	7⅝	9¼	1.2	8¼	9¼	1.1
20% (32)	30	⅝	2	3.2	2⅛	2	0.9	—	—	—
	25	2⅜	7	2.9	4¼	7	1.6	5⅜	7	1.3
	20	6⅜	12	1.9	7⅝	12	1.6	8¼	12	1.4
50% (40)	30	⅝	10	16.0	2⅛	10	4.7	—	—	—
	25	2⅜	15	6.3	4¼	15	3.5	5⅜	15	2.8
	20	6⅜	20	3.1	7⅝	20	2.6	8¼	20	2.4

dramatic as expected. The effect of small moves in the stock on the option is best seen by a variation of the break-even calculation. In this calculation, the price movement of the stock necessary to double the price of the option at expiration is calculated. To arrive at this price, the cost of the option is simply doubled and added to the strike price. The logic is as follows. At its expiration a call price will decline to the intrinsic value. Thus the stock price must advance to the extent that it will invest the option with a value of twice the initial purchase price over and above the strike price. If the common rises to this figure by expiration, the option will have doubled in value, thereby effecting a 100 percent return on investment. Next, this price increase of the common is divided by the initial price of the common to come up with the percent increase in the common to double each option price. Table 14 summarizes these calculations.

The results of the "double-your-money" approach are quite different from those derived by looking at reward/risk alone. For relatively small changes in stock price, the very deep-in-the-money options—those that have little or no premium in their price because their price is almost all intrinsic value—are *never* attractive. With the common bracketed by the 30 and 25 options, the Nw A 20 option is deeply in the money. By being deep in the money, it is the highest priced. Consequently, the stock must move the greatest percentage for this option to show a profit.

Secondly, the safest options, which require the least stock advance to show the best profit, are often those with a strike price just below the current common price. The Nw A 25s, regardless of the expiration date, were the most probable winners on the date the analysis was made.

At this point, one last dimension needs to be introduced—the element of time. The probability that an option price will double in one month is patently much less than the probability that it will double in four months, and still less again than the chance of its doubling in seven months. The more time, the greater the likelihood that the expected event will occur. Given enough time, even the end of the world will most assuredly come.

TABLE 14

Percent Move of Common to Double Option Price

Northwest Airline CBOE Options

(common @ 26⅝)

Strike Price	October 1 Mo. Left			January 4 Mo. Left			April 7 Mo. Left		
	Common Price to Double Option	Option Price	Percent Common Change	Common Price to Double Option	Option Price	Percent Common Change	Common Price to Double Option	Option Price	Percent Common Change
30	31¼	1¼	17.4	34¼	4¼	28.6	—	—	—
25	29¾	4¾	11.7	33½	8½	25.8	35¾	10¾	34.2
20	32¾	12¾	23.0	35¼	15¼	32.4	36½	16½	37.0

TABLE 15

Percent Move Per Month of Common to Double Option Price

Northwest Airline CBOE Options

(common @ 26⅝)

Strike Price	October 1 Mo. Left			January 4 Mo. Left			April 7 Mo. Left		
	Common Price to Double Option	Option Price	Percent Common Change Per Mo.	Common Price to Double Option	Option Price	Percent Common Change Per Mo.	Common Price to Double Option	Option Price	Percent Common Change Per Mo.
30	31¼	1¼	17.4	34¼	4¼	7.1	—	—	—
25	29¾	4¾	11.7	33½	8½	6.4	35¾	10¾	4.9
20	32¾	12¾	23.0	35¼	15¼	8.1	36½	16½	5.3

Table 15 reflects the impact of this increased probability over time by dividing the "percent move to double option price" in Table 14 by the remaining months of option life.

Viewed in this perspective, the longer options require a much lower percent move *per month* for the common to turn a handsome 100 percent profit. If price moves normally followed steady upward trends, this type of presentation would be most representative. In that price moves frequently occur rather dramatically and then settle down to a period of relative stability, the percent move per month for the common stock index is not wholly accurate. Nonetheless, this approach is one way to acknowledge the probabilistic advantage of having more time. As in Table 14, which was unadjusted for the time factor, the option with the strike price just below the stock price at the time the option is bought is still the most attractive option to buy from a short-term leverage standpoint.

Of course, time is money, particularly in options. The farther out the option, the higher the premium. It is interesting to note, however, that the more time one buys, the less it costs per unit. It's like a volume discount. The premium cost per month for six months is always much less than the cost per month for the first one to three months.

The price history of Atlantic Richfield during the last half of 1973 demonstrates the advantage of the long-term option.

TABLE 16
Selected Price History of Atl Rich 80

		July		October		January	
	Common	Option	Change	Option	Change	Option	Change
7/2/73	82½	4¾		10		13½	
7/31/73	86¾	6¾	2	10⅝	⅝	14½	1
10/29/73	108			28¾	18⅛	30⅛	15⅝
1/2/74	110⅞		_____		_____	31¾	1⅝
Cum. Gain			2		18¾		18¼

If a trader had become interested in the potential of Atlantic Richfield at the beginning of July 1973 and had bought the July call, he would have made $200 less commissions when the call expired. That's a 42 percent return on his investment of $475 plus commissions. Working with the $25 minimum commission figure, the investment would have been $500; the return $175; and the return on investment, 35 percent—with still a month to run. These much higher rates of return would have been affected only negligibly by the commission costs.

At this point, the most significant difference between the OTC and CBOE markets is quite obvious. To take profits in any one of the Atlantic Richfield calls, all the speculator had to do was sell the option. There was no capital required for exercising; no large commissions based on the underlying stock had to be paid. The sole cost incurred is the relatively nominal commission based on the price of the option.

If the same trader had become enamored with Exxon instead of Atlantic Richfield, the dark side of long-term trading would have manifested itself.

TABLE 17

Selected Price History of Exxon 100

		July		October		January	
	Common	Option	Change	Option	Change	Option	Change
7/2/73	98¼	1¾		5⅞		8	
7/31/73	95¾	nom.	−1¾	3⅞	−2	6½	−1½
10/29/73	96½			nom.	−3⅞	4½	−2
1/2/74	96½					1½	−3
Cum. Loss			−1¾		−5⅞		−6½

The losses speak for themselves. The longer-term options, while somewhat immune to the short-term swings in the common, also provide the opportunity to lose more money.

The whole analysis boils down to this. The cheapest options provide the greatest rewards for the risk if the stock makes a spectacular move upwards. On the other hand, if the move is much more modest, those options indicated by the "double-your-money" analysis are safer and will possibly yield a profit where none could be had from the cheaper options. The longer options are the cheapest per unit of time and, while costing more, have more time in which to become profitable. However, if the stock drops and stays down, everyone loses. Those owning the longer options lose the most. The former is betting $1 at 50-to-1 odds; the latter is betting $5 at 10-to-1 odds.

Short-Term Option Trading

Buying options for the long pull—conventional long-term trading —ignores the most attractive attribute of the Chicago Board Options Exchange: *liquidity*. Hardly any resale market existed before; the CBOE trades every day. While the market can be thin in certain unpopular options, there are competitive market makers assigned to always making a market in every option approved for trading. Undoubtedly, market depth will improve as volume increases and the exchange matures. If the stock market or a particular stock turns weak, the option owner does not have to ride it down. He can get out just as if he owned the stock and salvage some part of his capital for another day. This flexibility provides more profit opportunity for the short-term trader than for the relatively long-term position trader. The sooner the option speculator learns to appreciate this advantage and incorporates it into his trading strategy, the more profitable his operations will be.

Trading calls on the CBOE is like no other previous activity because these options are absolutely unique. As has already been amply demonstrated, the calls have all the leverage, with the concomitant limited risk, of the antecedent conventional OTC options.

Primarily because of the liquidity factor, the CBOE calls also have the characteristics of short-term warrants. Just like warrants, they can be readily bought and sold. In addition, unlike the OTC options, the CBOE options have a standard strike price and expiration date. These are comparable to a warrant's exercise price and expiration date. Also unlike OTC options, those calls on cash-paying stocks do not have their strike prices reduced by the amount of the dividend. Warrants are also not adjusted. Lastly, the relationship between premium, remaining life, stock price/strike price is virtually identical to the comparable warrant factors. The only nonsubstantive difference is that calls are written by individuals while warrants are issued by the parent corporation. In essence, however, CBOE calls and short-term warrants are identical.

Not only a call and simultaneously a warrant, CBOE options have several remarkable similarities to commodity futures contracts. The multiple CBOE option expiration dates are very much like the futures market multiple delivery months. The number of outstanding option contracts are referred to as open interest, just as are the futures contracts. This is most logical, since both options and futures are contracts between parties specifying the terms of some future transaction. At the end of each expiration month (delivery month in the futures), the option may either be exercised, closed out, or allowed to expire. Unlike options, futures contracts don't expire. In the futures market, the commodity must either be delivered or the contract closed out. Lastly, CBOE options have many of the same trading possibilities, such as spreads and cash hedges, as do futures.

Any instrument as unique and peculiar as the CBOE call can be traded in ways that are unfamiliar and yet very appropriate for its nature. By far the most profitable option trading technique is the one which accommodates a commodity futures orientation within a framework of shifting leverage. The commodity futures contract leverage springs from the possibility of very large price movements relative to the amount of money put into the position. Option leverage, while also keyed to the same small investment required, springs from the price relationship between the stock price and the strike price. In those cases where there are multiple strike prices such as the Brunswick 15s, 20s, and 25s, the leverage of each option changes as the stock price approaches each strike price. Several examples will be presented later.

The successful commodity trader operates from a set of principles quite different from those usually employed by the stock or conventional option trader. In the first place, the selection of any given contract month has no *necessary* inherent meaning. The only significance an expiration month has for a trader might come from some fundamental consideration, such as the beginning or end of a season or crop year, expected relief or tightness of supply, etc. In any major move, if one trading month goes up, they all go up, and vice versa. While the differences between the months might vary because of one of the above fundamental factors, the trend will be the same for all.

Next, a commodity trader will put his money where the action is. Clearly recognizable fundamental and technical factors have small value unless the price will move. Indeed, a solid, stable situation is anathema for both an option and commodity trader. The trader wants, and must have, a volatile market. Unfortunately, until the CBOE is allowed to make a market for put options, one can get volatiled to death with calls in a serious downward price break. Of course, such is not the case in commodities where the short side is not much less favored than the long side. The option trader's protection must come from a good defensive strategy coupled with the limited liability of the option. Commodity traders get margin calls; an option buyer never does.

The most important rule of commodity trading can also be applied to short-term option trading. "Cut your losses and let your profits run." The option holder can never lose more than he must initially put up. But the name of the game is to make money, not to lose capital. It has long been recognized that OTC option buyers tend to lose money overall. The SEC study published in 1961 observed that only 43 percent of all the OTC call options it included in its report were exercised. This included all those exercised at no profit or to minimize a loss. Logic insists that it will be a better policy to expect one reasonable profit to offset a series of small losses than to have to have one exceptional killing to offset a series of complete losses. While an option trader should never devote more than a modest portion of his capital to option trading, he should treat each dollar so deployed as if it were his last. By so doing, he will never have to dip into his reserves when he wants to pyramid a winning position.

So much for the principles. Now to the nitty-gritty. The option crap shooter should limit his attention to the nearby options. Both the percent premium of the underlying stock and absolute dollar expenditure are the least for the shorter options. Also the liquidity is greatest in these options. Generally, the most distant option seldom accounts for more than 10 percent of the total trading volume and open interest. The most nearby and the midlength option account for the balance, with the nearest option responsible for 40 to 50 percent of the volume. Whether this is a chicken-or-the-egg proposition is difficult to determine. Is the greatest volume in the nearbys because that's where the liquidity is, or are the nearbys liquid because that's where the interest is? My judgment on the matter is that the greatest interest is in the nearby options simply because they are the cheapest in absolute dollars to the buyer and not necessarily because there is a rational plan for trading these options on a short-term basis.

The first move a trader would make would be to survey the field. If he had certain specific companies and their options in mind, he would zero in on these. Otherwise, he would be wise to look them all over to find the best buys. Table 18 lists a few randomly selected options for comparative purposes.

Both the stock prices and options prices have been arbitrarily taken from October 2, 1973. When making a survey for his own use, the trader would obviously use the most current prices. First, the number of points the common must move for the option to double in price at expiration would be figured. Then, the "pay-out" percent relative to the common price would be worked out.

TABLE 18

100 Percent Payout for Selected CBOE Options

Company		Stock Price 10/2/73	Oct. Option Price	Stock Price to Double Option	Stock Change For 100% Payout		β	Req'd Change β
					points	%		
Nw A	30	26⅝	⅝	31¼	4⅝	17.4	1.67	10.4
	25		2⅜	29¾	3⅛	11.7		7.0
	20		6⅜	32¾	6⅛	23.0		13.8
Pennz	25	23⅞	1 1/16	27⅛	3¼	13.6	1.37	9.9
	20		3¾	27½	3⅝	15.2		11.1
Exxon	100	95½	⅞	101¾	6¼	6.5	.83	7.8
	90		6¼	102½	12½	13.1		15.8
Upjohn	100	84¾	1 1/16	101⅜	16⅝	19.6	1.0	19.6
	85		4⅛	93¼	8½	10.0		10.0
	75		12	99	14¼	16.8		16.8

This figure provides a way of comparing options that are deep-in-the-money with no premium attached to those that are way out-of-the-money and are all premium. The option that requires the least common price increase in order to achieve a 100-percent payout is usually the most attractive, because it has the best mathematical odds.

Referring to Table 18, it is seen that the best leveraged options would be the Nw A 25, the Pennz 25, the Exxon 100, and the Upjohn 85. In some cases, the most likely option is the one with a strike price just below the common price; in others, the one with the strike price just above the common. Generally there is no hard and fast rule without checking through the calculations.

Presumably the buyer has some idea in mind of what stock he thinks is going to make an upward move. As has been said repeatedly, the stock must have volatility. The fundamental strength, soundness, and growth rate of the company don't amount to a hill of beans if the price of the stock doesn't respond to these realities. As an indicator of volatility, the beta (β) of each stock has been included in Table 18. This index, taken from *Value Line,* is an indication of a particular stock's volatility compared to the market as a whole. However, it has no direction associated with it. There is no positive or negative beta. Consequently, a high beta can be taken to be as much a sign of great potential downward movement as up.

As will all indices, the beta index is calculated from past price changes. However, if one could forecast the future beta factor and its direction for a given stock, a perfect mechanical system could be developed to pick the option winners. Nonetheless, by dividing the percent stock movement required for a 100 percent option payout by the beta factor for the respective stock, a common denominator would be generated that could theoretically rate the attractiveness of all the options on all the stocks. In Table 18 the Exxon 100 declined in attractiveness because of the comparative lethargy of Exxon common, while the Nw A 25 dramatically improved because of Northwest Airline's historical ebullience.

Unfortunately, while mathematics is an exact science, calculable to infinity, speculation is a grand art. Included in that art is judgment, astuteness, and a good measure of luck. Every man is left to his own devices to pick a winning stock. But once the bet is placed (and the analysis in Table 18 points out the best odds), there are several trading practices that will help bring in a winner.

Never (or hardly ever) *let an option expire.* If the price of your call heads south, sell it! Use either a sell stop or a mental stop, but get out. There is no reason that your losers have to be 100 percent losers. By cutting your losses you will have some risk capital left to buy into a more favorably leveraged situation later on. The only circumstances under which one should not liquidate is when the commission costs (minimum of $25) would virtually eat up all the proceeds.

There is no specific rule about where to place the stop. It must be close enough to prevent a massive loss, yet far enough so that the normal and random variations in price won't trigger the stop and unnecessarily close out a sound position. Observation of the price movements of both the common and the selected option will give some feel for the "normal" fluctuation. Charts of the underlying stock and option can be very valuable in helping one to establish a guideline for each option.

One good example will demonstrate the advantages of this approach. During the summer of 1973, Brunswick began a rally upwards from its low for the year of 13¾. On the last trading day in October, when the Brunswick October options expired, Brunswick had risen to 25. That same day the next nearest-by January options were selling for the following prices:

BRUNSWICK (10/29/73)

Common Price	Strike Price	Jan. Option	% Common Move for 100% Option Payout
25	25	3⅛	25%
	20	6¾	34%
	15	10⅝	45%

With three months left before expiration, the January 25 option was selling for a hefty premium of 12½ percent for the three months, or 50 percent on an annualized basis. Yet, the common was certainly trending in the right direction and the January 25 option was not only the cheapest option available, but also the one requiring the least common advance to show a good profit.

As circumstances would have it, the end of October signaled the Mid-East war, the oil embargo, and the birth of the energy crisis. The resulting utter chaos decimated the stock market. In four weeks the Dow Jones Industrial Average plummeted more than 170 points. By November 28, 1973 Brunswick common had collapsed to 13⅝. The options followed suit.

BRUNSWICK (11/28/73)

Common Price	Strike Price	Jan. Option	% Common Move for 100% Option Payout
13⅝	25	¼	87%
	20	¾	58%
	15	1¹³⁄₁₆	37%

If the January 25 option owner had held on, his investment would have shrunk from $312.50 to $25. Worse than that, he would have no realistic hope of recovery. In the two months of life left, the common would have to advance 87 percent just to double the remaining $25 to $50. To recapture this original $312.50, Brunswick would have to advance 106 percent. Fat chance!

However, with an intelligently placed stop, at least $200 could have been salvaged from the Jan. 25. If the Brunswick speculator were still enthusiastic, he could buy back a position in the Jan. 15 and still have some change left over. While the Jan. 25 was virtually worthless, the Jan. 15 had some profit possibilities. Either way, the speculator would have been far better off by having sold out.

Rolling with the shifting leverage is also a superior strategy in an up market. The idea is to buy the best situated nearby option and, when it approaches expiration, sell it and buy the best situated upcoming nearby option. In essence, the trader is "rolling over" his profitable position as the most nearby option expires, each time reinvesting in a cheaper, better leveraged option. Sperry Rand, in the latter part of 1973 (Table 19), is a good example.

TABLE 19
Sperry Rand CBOE Price History

Date	Common	Strike Price	Options		
			July	October	January
7/2	39½	40	1¾	4¼	6
7/31	46	45		4⅞	6¼
		40	6	8	9¾
10/29	55⅞	55			5⅛
		45		10	13
		40		15⅜	16¾

Table 20 recaps the comparative profit capabilities of "rolling over" versus "buying and holding" long term.

Buying either the midterm October or most deferred January option would have resulted in a respectable profit over the period used in the table. As might be expected, the October had a better return because it cost less. The best performer would have been rolling over the nearby. If the July 40 option was sold before it expired, there was enough money received to buy the October 45 and still have 1⅛ points left over. In calculating the profit, the most conservative route was used. The 1⅛ points from July were added to the October selling price of 10, and the original cost of 1¾ subtracted from that total to come up with the profit of 9⅜ points. This same calculation could also result in an astronomical return on investment if the 1⅛ points cash generated on July 31 were used to reduce the original investment of 1¾ points to ⅝. The profit would still be the same 9⅜ points and the return would have been 1500 percent. Let this simple instance caution the reader that exactly opposing positions can often be equally justified with the very same set of numbers.

TABLE 20

Recap of "Rolling-Over" Sperry Rand Option

Strategy	Date	Buy	Sell	Profit	Return
1. Buy Jan. 40	7/2	6			
Sell Jan. 40	10/29		16¾	10¾	179%
Investment		6			
2. Buy Oct. 40	7/2	4¼			
Sell Oct. 40	10/29		15⅜	11⅛	262%
Investment		4¼			
3. Buy July 40	7/2	1¾			
Sell July 40	7/31		6		
Buy Oct. 45	7/31	4⅞			
Sell Oct. 45	10/29		10	9⅜	536%
Investment		1¾			

As is so often the case in this world, many things don't always work right. If the reader will refer back to Table 16 (Selected Price History of Atlantic Richfield), he will see that the "roll-over" with that stock at the prevailing option price was a very poor candidate. If the July 80 option was sold at expiration and the money applied to buying the October 80, additional capital would have been required. Instead of pyramiding the profits on winnings, the only thing that would have been pyramided was the investment. And the risk!

Rolling over works when the trader can take some of his money out each time he rolls over his position. He must be able to sell an in-the-money option and in turn reposition himself with an option that is cheaper because it has less intrinsic value. This he can do with stock options that have an ascending scale of strike prices. On the roll-over date of July 31, Atlantic Richfield had only one strike price for all its options and consequently it could not be traded to take advantage of shifting leverage. As the CBOE grows and time passes, new strike prices will have to be introduced because of stock prices moving up and down. This should enhance the opportunities for pyramiding profits.

Hedging with CBOE Options

CBOE options can be used in two types of hedges: one is intermarket, the other intramarket. The intermarket hedge, an option offsetting a stock position, is currently one-sided, because the CBOE deals only in calls thus far. Consequently, the position to be hedged with a CBOE call can be only a short sale of the common. The purpose of the call is to make money to offset the short side losses if the stock rises instead of falls. The selection of the proper call with which to hedge would be made in the same way that one would buy insurance. Since one doesn't expect to have to use the insurance, the hedger would be attracted to an option that has little or no intrinsic value. However, for the insurance to provide price protection, the call must start moving up with the stock without too much lag. A 100 option on an $80 stock sold short would be inadequate insurance. A 60 option on the same stock would be too expensive. The best buy for a hedge would be an 80 option on an $80 stock.

The intramarket hedge is called a "spread." This term is taken directly from the commodities futures market. In spread, one is both long and short different options on the same common stock. A long position is equivalent to a bought option. A short position is the same as selling or writing an option. The ratio between the long and the short does not have to be one-to-one. The individual situation might dictate that long 3 and short 1 would be the soundest hedge or spread.

There is a wide variety of different types of spreads. There can be strike price spreads, in which one will buy a call and then write a call at a different strike price. Then there is an expiration spread, in which one might buy the nearby and write the deferred —all at the same strike price. Finally, there are the combinations of both strike price and expiration date. Theoretically, one might be long XYZ April 40s and short XYZ July 45s.

Profits from spreads are generated from small differences in prices for different options. The profits are relatively small—maybe 1 to 1½ points—but so also is the risk. These differences in prices occur because each option has some amount of premium over and above the option's intrinsic value associated with it. This premium will vary from none at all to 100 percent when the option has no intrinsic value. The immutable law of options—that all premium will disappear at expiration—drives each option price a slightly different amount. The idea of the spread is to establish a position that will be profitable and to safely "milk" the premium out of the options as it nears expiration.

The future of spreading rests with the SEC. The viability of spreading depends on the cost of doing business. Since the profit from spreads is relatively modest, the activity is attractive only as long as the margin requirements are low. At its inception, the CBOE started with low margin requirements, more in line with those for commodities than with those for stocks. However, the SEC and the NYSE have been pressing for stiffer and more uniform requirements because of the repercussions of the Goldstein-Samuelson naked option swindle.

The cash needed for the long side of a spread is no more than the cost of the option. The short side of the spread (in which the spreader sells an option and is paid money by the buyer) must be secured by 100 shares of the outright stock, 100 shares of margined stock, or by cash. If the spreader has to buy the stock outright, or even on margin (in which he must put up between 40 to 50 percent of the value of the underlying stock), spreading becomes rather unattractive because of the relatively large amount of money tied up for a small profit. At the beginning of 1974, the CBOE's cash margin requirements for selling a call as part of a spread were $500 for a stock selling for less than 50, $1,000 for a stock with a price between 50 and 100, and $1,500 for a stock priced over 100. If the SEC pressures the CBOE to raise margin requirements on the naked short leg of a spread to the same as those for the short sale of the underlying stock, the major activity in spreading will probably disappear.

Summary

Because of the unique characteristics of CBOE call options, their trading possibilities are limited only by the imagination. However, their principal mode of use falls into two broad categories. Holding options long term, usually up to the expiration date, follows the pattern of conventional option techniques. Short-term trading with an eye to shifting leverage is more in the spirit of commodities trading.

When buying an option to hold for its whole life, the selection of the least expensive option constitutes the least risky approach. Because of the lesser money at risk, a major upward move of the stock yields the greatest percentage gains. However, the likelihood of realizing these profits is much less probable.

The most probable selection is indicated by the "double your money" analysis. Usually this analysis points to the option with a strike price just below current stock price as the most attractive. This more attractive option also has frequently a somewhat higher dollar risk.

The very deep-in-the-money options are never attractive because they require the greatest number of dollars at risk and need a large stock price rise for even a reasonable return.

For long-term holding, the longer options are cheap in terms of the amount of time purchased. They are also less affected by temporary adverse price movements in the common. The longest call with a strike price selected by "double your money" analysis should be the one purchased.

The speculator who is interested in short-term trading possibilities is better off in the nearby options, where he is assured a good market liquidity. The lower price of the nearby options will also increase his odds for a profitable operation by lowering his risk per trade.

He should hardly ever let an option expire. That is wasteful laziness. The short-term trader will always place sell stops, either actual or mental, on all the calls he buys. He will treat each of the dollars he trades as if it were his last. By using this strategy, he will have some capital remaining after an unforeseen market break and consequently be able to reenter the market under more advantageous terms.

As the price of the common under option approaches one strike price and moves away from another, the price leverage of the options shifts. The short-term trader can roll over a profitable position on expiration, take some money out, and put on a new position in the upcoming expiration date option at a higher strike price. By this maneuver, he can increase his leverage and decrease his investment.

The short-term trader never *has to* trade. If the leverage on two option possibilities is a standoff, he can wait a few days for the scales to tip one way or the other. Or there might be a stock that is very strong but that does not have an option with any satisfactorily leveraged strike price. Like the long-term trader, he always looks to the fundamental and technical strengths of the underlying stock. However, by being more aware of the unique attributes of CBOE calls, he will adjust his timing to reflect a realistic appraisal of reward/risk and leverage probabilities.

4

The Repercussions

W<small>HEN</small> the Chicago Board of Trade tried to drum up pre-opening interest for the Chicago Board Options Exchange, its "flying squad" was received with skeptical apathy. The old options hands thought the structure of fixed strike prices and fixed expiration dates was too complicated for the speculators to comprehend. As a matter of fact, they weren't even sure they understood how this new exchange would work. Then to top it off, they questioned how a non-securities oriented exchange such as the Chicago Board of Trade could ever fathom the intricacies of the securities business. Assuming it could, the final backhand shot was: "Nobody will ever make a buck setting up a whole exchange just to trade options."

Once the SEC finished fiddling and diddling and authorized the beginning of a "pilot" market, the trade publications picked up the chant. The July 15, 1973 issue of *Forbes* ran an article entitled "Chicago Board Options: Under Water?" This piece cleverly pointed out the very tired saw that in a down market, option holders can lose a large percentage of their money while stockholders lose only a small percentage. The main thrust of the article was that option buyers rarely make money. The fact that the option buyer has much less at risk and the fact that bought calls might well have been one side of a short sale hedge were not mentioned. Conceding that the three-month-old baby exchange might be precocious, *Forbes* nonetheless implied a foreboding future.

As soon as the market turned up vigorously in September 1973, other members of the financial press jumped to the other side of the fence. A November 1973 *Fortune* article, "The Values in Options," and "Primer on Options" in *Barron's* November 12, 1973, drew attention to the highly leveraged paper profits that had been reaped from the upturn in the underlying common stocks. All the while espousing the usual caveats—"beware being an option buyer" and "don't spend the mortgage money on options" —the tenor of the articles was absolutely enthusiastic. The financial fraternity, at least, seemed to feel that even *good* news is occasionally fit to print.

What's Happening Now

People making money in a good market and losing money in a bad market—that was certainly not news. The real news was that from the summer to the fall of 1973, both the open interest and volume doubled on the "pilot run." The CBOE's October volume (266,000 calls on just 32 stocks) equaled the entire previous *year's* volume on the OTC market. That was news. The likelihood that the open interest might climb to 1,000,000 contracts—equivalent to 100,000,000 shares of stock—by the end of 1974 will also be news if it happens.

Needless to say, the OTC market was initially stunned. Nobody could believe that what did happen could happen. However, being pragmatists above all, the OTC option dealers didn't fight it. Using pre-eminent good sense, many dealers took out memberships on the CBOE. They recognized that the OTC market wasn't going to disappear overnight, if ever. After all, the CBOE deals in calls on only 32 stocks. There is still quite a market for straddles, puts, and calls on the thousands of other stocks traded. In all likelihood, as option markets grow and proliferate, the OTC business will concentrate on special situations, which do not have enough broad interest to support a liquid market.

Only one group is really having trouble adapting to the success of the CBOE. The SEC let a little kitty cat into the house one night and the next morning found a glowering tiger at the foot of its bed. The "pilot run," which was supposed to allow the agency time to evaluate the results, just got too big to hold in the cage. With typical bureaucratic impuissance, the SEC has tried to starve it to death to see if it might shrivel—and barring that, to stuff the beast back into the cage.

At the onset of the experiment, an orderly expansion of stocks under option was envisioned. The original list of 16 was opened up to 32 stocks, and then frozen. Whereas the first additions had been effected by occasional administrative fiat, in early 1974, hearings were required to decide if more should be added. Several other exchanges desirous of getting a piece of the option action were stalled and stalled. Again hearings, but not answers.

When the Mid-East war pulled the props out from under the market in November 1973, the SEC immediately announced— the only time a federal agency will move fast is to stop somebody from doing something, a move that is almost always precipitously premature—a new rule to "cool" the volume in naked options. It is this same rule (requiring much larger margins for writing naked) that could completely squelch option spreading. In making the announcement, Mr. Lee A. Pickard, head of the SEC Trading and Markets Division, said: "We are very concerned about the increased attention in the options market. There is a pressing need for greater consumer protection in that area."[1] Obviously, the consumer protection in mind was to prevent naked option writers from going broke.

The SEC has also laid an injunction on any option holder owning more than 1,000 options on any one common stock. The purpose of this edict was ostensibly twofold, although only one reason really makes sense. The most logical rationale for the restriction on the size of option holdings is to prevent a cornering, with the subsequent manipulation, of the underlying common. The second reason was to prevent the public from overspeculating and getting in too deep. This explanation has an unauthentic ring to it. First, when an option buyer puts down his cash, that's the extent of his liability. There can be no further calls for cash. And obviously, he had to have the cash in the first place before he could spend it. Second, a limit of 1,000 calls is certainly not going to protect the average option speculator. With cheap calls selling for between 1 to 8 points, or $100 to $800 each, the injunction prevents a speculator from spending more than somewhere between $100,000 to $800,000 on one stock. No average speculator, he.

The evidence indicates that the SEC is scared. And rightly so. It has opened up a Pandora's Box of implications that it neither fully comprehends nor can control. Consequently, the agency is trying to act as circumspectly as possible. The hope is that caution does not lead to paralysis.

The option buyers and writers have been anything but overly cautious. Judging by the phenomenal growth rate of both volume and open interest, both buyers and sellers are knocking one another over to get into the game. As of early 1974, there has been no flattening out of growth and no foreseeable plateau is in sight. As the carnival barker cries, on spinning the wheel of fortune, "Around she goes, and where she stops, nobody knows."

How well have the option buyers made out? It all depends.

---

[1] *Wall Street Journal*, November 29, 1973.

From midsummer of 1973 to the end of the year, the stock market was initially up and then resoundingly down. In midsummer, there were 23 options being traded on the CBOE. From the beginning to the end of the same six-month period, the stock underlying these options moved as follows: 5 issues up with 3 sharply so, 8 down with 4 sharply so, and 10 virtually unchanged. Generally, the market has been far better for the writer than for the buyer. Of course, this is true only if the respective writer or buyer were active in every issue. Since individuals most often will make judgments and thereby concentrate on some options and not others, the profitability for each option buyer depends on what he bought. If he bought the right options, he made a lot of money. Strange, but that's just the way the stock market works. Except that on the CBOE there were at least 5 winners out of 23.

My judgment of the matter is that a great deal more speculators probably lost money buying options than those who made money. One can mathematically demonstrate that it takes intelligent selection to make money buying options and virtually no sense at all to make money writing options. Therefore, most people lost money buying options.

One observation confirms this logic. Throughout the awesome November 1973 break in the market, the open interest on the CBOE consistently increased. This indicates that very few longs liquidated. If they had been cutting their losses, the open interest would have declined or at least stabilized on balance. Rather, the longs just watched their option money go down the drain day after day. Combining unfortunate option selection and foolish trading practices will guarantee consistent losses.

One benefit has accrued to all option buyers since the early days of the CBOE. The cost of calls as a percentage of the underlying stock has decreased. As yet it is unclear as to whether this is more or less permanent, because there are a large number of writers competing in a free marketplace for the attention of a lesser number of buyers. It could also be a temporary reflection of the clouded economic prospects for 1975. Only time will tell.

What's in the Cards

The speculators and the institutions have resoundingly cast their votes concerning whether they want and will use an open market for options. The other exchanges, anxious to get into the business, have expressed their confidence in the viability of such a market. The SEC is in the wings, pondering what this all means.

The SEC's reluctance to blunder on seems to revolve around three questions and/or doubts. Will an options market (not just the CBOE, but possibly a national options market) draw speculative capital out of the stock market? If such an options market is not detrimental to the satisfaction of any existing capital requirements, does it serve a legitimate, useful purpose? Lastly, even if both answers are yes, could the options market evolve into some kind of speculative monster?

Taking these issues in order, the first concern is that money that might normally be used to buy the stocks of new speculative companies would be diverted into options. Since one of the primary purposes of the stock market is to provide capital for new ventures, this is a significant worry. However, viewing the options market as a threat to the ability to raise new capital is like a prospective bride fearing all unattached women. You either compete or you don't. No amount of force is going to force a yes from the groom. Speculative capital flows toward vehicles that are perceived to be profitable opportunities. If the new issues that are offered are unappealing or overly risky, those speculative dollars will be spent on gold, or works of art, or commodities, or even options. There is no way that speculative money will finance an operation to which the speculators are indifferent.

Since the options market cannot be detrimental to other financial needs—which would go a-begging regardless of whether there were such a market—the next question is whether the market serves any useful purpose. Is the options market frivolous, like a race track, or a crap game? Or does it fill some worthwhile economic or financial need?

The problem of capital allocation goes a great deal deeper than whether new issue needs will be met. The problem rests with the whole stock market. On December 21, 1973, Westinghouse announced that, due to various heavy losses in several subsidiaries, the projected 1973 net income would probably be some 15 percent less than the previous year. Westinghouse dropped from 32¼ to 24⅜ in one day of trading of more than ½ million shares. This 24 percent drop in the stock of one of America's largest, soundest corporations erased $697,685,620 in equity value. That's more than two-thirds of a *billion* dollars in *one* corporation in *one* day. The institutions killed themselves and the stock when they all tried to get out through the same knothole. Since this debacle, there have been several similar episodes with other stocks, such as Combustion Engineering and Polaroid, to name a few.

Liquidity is the stock market's problem. There are too many generals and no soldiers. In recent years the character of the stock market has changed markedly. While the ownership of equity is still quite broad, the institutions have increasingly dominated the trading. Owning perhaps 30 percent of all the shares listed on the NYSE, the institutions account for more than two-thirds of all the trading activity. The upshot of this concentration of investment decisions is that a very few men are determining the value of the savings of millions of investors. Because of the impact of these large blocks of shares on both price and trading action, the market for stocks is becoming more volatile and less liquid. This is clearly not a public good. The public has not only left the new issue market; they have deserted the whole battlefield. Brokerage houses are folding because the public is not buying. By raising the commission rates, they have driven out the last of the die-hard traders.

The options market can attack the problem of illiquidity both directly and indirectly. With a list of only 32 stocks, the benefits still are quite minor. If the list is expanded to include a broad segment of the major corporations, *and puts are allowed to trade,* the options market can go a long way to mitigate some of the worst damage of precipitous price movements that are the direct result of illiquidity.

Easy access to a broad options market provides a hedging

medium that option *buyers* can use to protect their portfolios against unexpected updrafts or downdrafts. Realistically, however, a predominate proportion of option buyers are not hedgers. They are out and out speculators.

Just the converse is true of option writers. By far the greatest number of writers are hedgers who use the option premium earned on their portfolio to offset declines in capital value. These persons, who manage both their own and large institutional funds, tend to be relatively conservative. They are also the same ones who can, and do, dump large blocks of stock when they have no other choice in a deteriorating market. They are one side of the illiquidity equation. It is their enormous buy or sell orders that hit the market devoid of a raft of small public orders that jolt market prices. A flourishing options market would be an income-earning alternative not now available.

Divestiture or investiture decisions would not need to be made in a crisis atmosphere, simply because the option writing program would continually be generating a cash cushion against adversity.

A broad-based options market would also offer other alternatives to an outright buy-or-sell decision. If an institution were overcommitted in a given security, it could reduce its position by writing calls in an up market or buying puts in a down market. By effecting delivery of the stock to either a call buyer or put writer, it could rebalance its portfolio without resorting to a massive selling campaign. If this same institution were interested in acquiring a large position in a stock, it could accomplish its purpose either by buying calls or by writing naked puts. A well-developed options market would be as invaluable for the institution as the futures market is for the hedging farmer. And history has proven that an effective hedging mechanism reduces price volatility—not the opposite.

The last concern of the SEC is whether a full-blown options market could turn into some kind of speculative monster. This question has caused the SEC to drag its feet on permitting other competitive call markets and the sale of puts.

There seem to be few doubts that a put market would be successful. The institutions are generally more desirous of originating straddles than calls. They can earn almost twice the premium on straddles as on calls without a commensurate increase in risk. By writing straddles, they would be generating a put option with every call. Any time there is a greater demand for calls than puts (which is usually the case), the converters could step in and convert puts into calls. This would keep supply and demand approximately in balance.

From the buyer's standpoint, he could combine a put and a call at any time to create a straddle. He would not be restricted to a one-sided market that could be profitable only if the market moved upward. The speculator would be getting a much fairer deal.

But what would happen if thousands upon thousands of speculators poured their money into the current list of 32 options? It is not beyond the realm of possibility that the CBOE open interest could reach 1,000,000 contracts by the end of 1974. That's equivalent to 100,000,000 million shares of the underlying stock. Generally, the monthly trading volume is about equal to the total open interest. Thus 1,000,000 open interest would indicate a monthly volume of 1,000,000. Divide the volume by 20 days per month, and the daily volume would be 50,000 calls per day traded, equivalent to 5,000,000 shares. If this projection is reasonably accurate, the option volume in equivalent shares would be more than *twice* the trading volume of the underlying stock. It would also be approximately 25 percent of volume traded on *all* the stocks on the New York Stock Exchange on any given day.

Doesn't that make it a monster without question? I believe not. Wall Street's biggest problem is that the public, the odd lotter, is out of the market. The option market is a place to which the public has come back; and the public is apparently willing to continue doing so. The public sees its risk as much less in options than in trying to crapshoot Wall Street. With the public in, there are hundreds of thousands of individuals reaching different decisions at different times, not a handful of fund managers trying to get through a knothole at one time.

As regards optioned shares trading in greater volume than the underlying stock's shares, such an anomaly poses no necessary threat of overspeculation. The same phenomenon regularly occurs in the commodities market. As an instance, in 1973 every bushel of soybeans grown changed hands more than ten times in the futures market. The crop was 1,282 million bushels. Futures contracts equivalent to 13,500 million bushels were traded on the Chicago Board of Trade. A large part of the reason for this great volume of trading stems from the multiple contract expiration dates within a one-year period. Hedgers, whether in the commodities or options market, quite often will establish and subsequently unwind hedges many times in the futures market while buying or selling the underlying commodities only once. An institution geared to writing short-term options for income on the CBOE can write four calls a year, equivalent to 400 shares, without ever once trading the 100 shares of underlying stock in its portfolio. The balance of the terrific volume arises from the activities of the thousands of short-term speculators who trade in and out daily, weekly, and monthly.

A broad-based options market would take over the pricing function from the stock market. This means that the public would assume the pricing function. Such an event would be an enormous public good. Stock prices would not fluctuate all over the map on one piece of news, because the options market introduces a vastly greater number of buyers and sellers with divergent opinions. The stock market would return to some semblance of an orderly, reasonably efficient financial institution. Since the stock market is the nation's major source of business capital, any "paper speculation" that aids the market function is consistent with public policy.

Here's how it would work. If a large number of the public on balance thought a stock was a good value, they would drive up the option price by their buying. At some point the premium would become so attractive that the institutions would buy the common stock and write call options against it. Their buying would in turn increase the price of the stock. This would be a self-fulfilling prophecy with the investing public making the prediction.

If the public thought a stock price too high, they would buy puts. Here again, as the option premium became attractive, the institutions would sell short the common and write puts. These short sales would tend to soak up any buying power for the stock, thereby leading to a lower stock price. Another prophecy fulfilled.

The mechanics of the relationship between an options market and the stock market described herein are greatly simplified. The myriad of associated problems would be real and difficult to tackle. Nonetheless, the SEC is currently presented with an unparalleled opportunity to improve imaginatively the health of the country's vital capital financing system. If past history is a reliable guide, there is at least a slim hope.

APPENDIX: The Mechanics of Options Buying

Anyone interested in options will probably already have a relationship with a stockbroker whose firm is a member of the Chicago Board Options Exchange as well as the Put and Call Brokers and Dealers Association, Inc. In the event one has no satisfactory connection, I would recommend that a broker be selected with the same care as one would use in choosing a family doctor. This man will certainly be making recommendations vital to one's financial health.

References from friends and associates can be a good place to start. Next, one should actually interview the prospective candidates. Equal attention should be given to the integrity of the individual broker and the services his firm offers. In evaluating a broker, the best plan is to explain to him both one's investing and one's speculative aims. If he understands and is sympathetic to the approach, and his firm can provide the necessary services, he would be a likely prospect.

Once the man and the brokerage house have been picked out, the next step would be to open an account. This simply requires filling out an application that supplies the broker with a brief history and credit references.

Normal procedure requires that an account must have enough money on deposit fully to cover any cash purchase at the time the purchase is made. Consequently, enough money would usually be paid in to the broker at the time the account is opened to satisfy any immediately planned trades. Since options can only be purchased in the cash account, the full price of the option would be required. If one were writing an option, either 100 shares of the securities involved, or 50 percent of the market value of the securities (the required initial margin in the fall of 1974), would have to be deposited. Oftentimes, after a long and satisfactory relationship, the broker will execute a trade with the stipulation that the required funds be sent in within five business days.

In either buying or selling options on the OTC market, it is customary for the seller to quote a price. The buyer may either accept, counter-offer, or refuse the offer. There is never any doubt about the authenticity of the prices.

When dealing on the CBOE, placing an order is an entirely different situation. This Chicago-based market is a composite of the pure auction market (such as the commodity futures market) and the "specialist" system used by the major stock exchanges. At any given moment, there might not always be buyers and sellers whose bids and offers are in line with a fair market value.

Rather than placing a "market" order either to buy or sell the specific option under consideration, under normal circumstances one would place a "limit" order. A market order to buy means that the purchase will be made at the next offering price, whether reasonable or not. A market order to sell means that the order will be executed at the next bid price, regardless of whether it is at or away from the market.

In markets that are either very thin or highly volatile, I would suggest that only limit orders be used. The CBOE, even though it has assigned market makers to assure relatively liquid markets, still occasionally suffers from very "jerky" trading. Frequently, the major stock exchanges have the same problem. A limit order is one that will be executed only at a price no worse than the one specified. A buy can be made only at the limit price or lower. A sale can be made only at the limit or higher price. In this way, the trader is assured that the trade price will be in line with his expectations. The limit order is protection against the occasional "ripoff" that can occur in a thin market.

Once one has a position, the problem of placing a stop loss order then comes into play. Of course, this consideration applies only to the CBOE. If one bought an option, he would place a sell stop at some price lower than the existing market. The logic is to sell out a position that is showing a loss to conserve as much money as possible. The individual speculator would establish in his own mind how much risk he was willing to take in buying the option and so set the price at which he would "bail out." If the price either declined or was offered down to the sell stop price, the order automatically would become a market order to sell. In line with the previous comments about thin markets, one can also place a sell stop limit order. Once the stop is triggered by a declining market, the order becomes an order to sell at the limit price or better. While this type of order will protect one from being "ripped off" when the stop is activated, it can also leave one at the dock in a rapidly decaying market.

The seller on the CBOE faces the same considerations. If one had sold a naked call and wanted protection from a runaway price advance, a buy stop or buy stop limit order would be entered at a price somewhat above the current market. If the price or bid advanced to the stop level, the order would be activated either to buy at the market or at the limit price specified by the order.

Glossary

Beta (β) An index measuring the sensitivity of a stock's price to overall fluctuations in the New York Stock Exchange's Composite Average. A beta of 1.5 indicates a stock tends to rise (or fall) 1.5 percent with a 1 percent rise (or fall) in the NYSE Composite Average.

Call Money Also, call loans. Money lent by banks to brokers, collateralized by securities and subject to repayment on demand.

Call Option A contract that entitles the owner to buy 100 shares of a stock at a stipulated price at any time during the period the option is in force.

Covering Also, buying in. A term used to describe the completion of a short sale transaction whereby the stock is bought on the open market and used to replace those shares borrowed and originally sold short.

Debit Balance An accounting total that represents the total charges (i.e., money borrowed from the broker) against a customer's margin account.

Debt Leverage The concept of borrowing money to buy securities. Any increase or decrease in the total value of the securities accrues to the borrower alone, not the lender.

Equity The net value of an account after all money borrowed from the broker is subtracted from the market value of the securities in the account.

In-the-Money A term used to describe an option that has intrinsic value. A call at 40 on a stock trading at 50 is in-the-money 10 points.

Intrinsic Value A measure of the value of an option or a warrant if immediately exercised.

Long A person who owns stock either outright or in a margin account. Also used as an adjective to describe outright ownership.

Maintenance Margin The minimum amount of equity required in a margin account. The current maintenance margin is an equity equal to or greater than 30 percent of the account's market value. If the equity falls below this level, either more money must be put up or the stock be sold out.

Margin The term used to describe buying securities when a portion of the purchase price is borrowed from the brokerage house. Specifically, the margin is the amount of money that the customer must put up when buying on credit.

Margin Call The request by a broker for more money to bring a margin account up to the minimum maintenance margin requirement.

Market Value The current value of all the securities held in a margin account.

Naked Call A call option originated by an option writer who does not own or buy the 100 shares of the stock on which the option is written, but rather leaves cash in his account as a surety that he will honor his contract.

Naked Put A put option originated by an option writer who does not sell short 100 shares of the stock on which the option is written, but rather leaves cash in his account as a surety that he will honor his contract.

Option Buyer The person who buys calls, puts, or any combination thereof.

Option Seller Also, option writer. The person who originates an option contract by promising to perform a certain obligation in return for the price of the option.

Out-of-the-Money A term used to describe an option that has a negative intrinsic value. A call at 40 on a stock trading at 30 is out-of-the-money 10 points.

Premium That portion of an option price that is in excess of the intrinsic value. In cases where the strike price and the stock price are the same, the total cost of the option is premium.

Put Option The right to sell 100 shares of a security at a fixed price at any time during the option period.

SEC The Securities Exchange Commission, a federal agency charged with regulating the securities industry.

Short A person who has sold securities he doesn't own, and who consequently has an obligation ultimately to repurchase a like amount of shares in the open market.

Short Sale Selling stock one doesn't own in anticipation of repurchasing the borrowed stock at a lower price. Under current regulations, the shares sold short must first be borrowed.

Spreads In the OTC option market, a spread is a put and a call option combination on the same stock with each option having a different strike price. In the CBOE market, a spread is the combination of buying a call and writing a call on a different strike price or expiration date option of the same stock.

Straddle   The combination of a put and call on the same stock with each option of the "double option" having the same strike price.

Strike Price   The price at which an option can be exercised.

Index